DAD H.
ENGINE SHED

Some childhood
railway reminiscences
of a
North Wales
shedmaster's son

by
Anthony J. Robinson
C. Eng., M.I.Mech.E.

THE OAKWOOD PRESS

British Library Cataloguing in Publication Data
A Record for this book is available from the British Library
ISBN 978 0 85361 707 5

Typeset by Oakwood Graphics.
Repro by PKmediaworks, Cranborne, Dorset.
Printed by Cambrian Printers, Aberystwyth, Ceredigion.

The North Wales shed masters in the early 1950s. *From left to right*: J.M. Dunn, Bangor; T.G. Dentith, Holyhead; C. Highett, Llandudno Jn; A.R. Ewer, Chester; J.E. Robinson, Mold Jn; J. Dicken, Birkenhead; Mr Lloyd, Rhyl.   *J.M. Dunn*

Front cover: J.E. Robinson standing in front of 'Royal Scot' class 4-6-0 No. 46115 *Scots Guardsman*. The locomotive was just about to leave Mold Junction shed when photographer Norman Kneale caught it; he persuaded my father to pose in front of it. It was probably the last time a 'Scot' graced the Chester-Holyhead line, the locomotive was withdrawn from Carlisle (Kingmoor) in August 1965.   *E.N. Kneale*

Rear cover, top: The 5.00 pm from Denbigh leaves Mold on the final day of passenger services, 28th April, 1962. The author is seen leaning out of the front compartment window. Note the substantial goods shed which was originally an engine shed of the Mold Railway.   *M. Mensing*

Rear cover, lower: Mold Junction's crank shaft-driven ex-LMS diesel shunter is seen on the ex-GWR Saltney Cop line. A Stanier '8F' class 2-8-0 passes above bound for Mold Junction on the down slow line.   *John Ryan*

Published by The Oakwood Press (Usk), P.O. Box 13, Usk, Mon., NP15 1YS.
E-mail: sales@oakwoodpress.co.uk
Website: www.oakwoodpress.co.uk

Contents

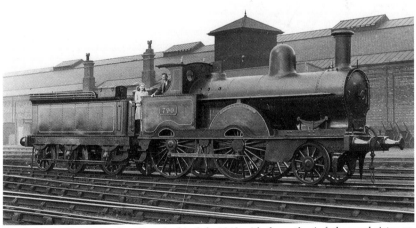

Hardwicke at Llandudno Junction shed in July 1948 with the author's father and sister on the footplate. It was the occasion of the centenary of the opening of the Chester & Holyhead Railway. Several locomotives, including this famous 'Jumbo' and the single-wheeler *Lady of the Lake*, were being prepared for a static exhibition in Conway goods yard. Max Dunn had been charged with setting up a display of artefacts in the nearby station waiting room.   *J.M. Dunn*

Introduction

What, one may ask, compels the writing of a tome dedicated to the working life of a parent who passed away over 40 years ago and who was not someone known to the general public in a way that most people could identify with? Indeed I have frequently asked myself this question during the past 10 years or so that I have been somewhat leisurely engaged in the researching and writing of this book. If there is a simple answer I suppose it is that losing my father at the age of 18 left me feeling cheated; as an Engineer and Manager himself he could have offered so much guidance during and after my apprentice and student years. He had a wealth of experience on which to draw and no doubt would have tried to guide me through some of the pitfalls that I personally experienced in the early part of my career in engineering and man management. To say that he was a hard working man would be an understatement in the extreme, this was a quality that he expected from myself during my school days and he was very economical with his praise should I (rarely) achieve anything worthwhile. My mother used to say that, 'Praise from your father is praise indeed!'

However, he did admit that he was immensely proud that I gained an engineering apprenticeship with one of the country's leading aircraft manufacturers and one of the last functions he attended was the signing of my indentures early in 1966. Looking back over my own experiences it began to emerge just how difficult his career and work life must have been. Who today could image someone in charge of over 200 men and 60-odd locomotives living in a council house and going to work on a bicycle! Working five full days a week plus Saturday and Sunday mornings and having to be on permanent standby day and night for breakdowns and, yes, for no extra pay at that! It has been written elsewhere that a typical shedmaster had to have the powers of judgement of Solomon, the ingenuity of Trevithick, the stubbornness of Stephenson, the leadership skills of Patton, the negotiating powers of Kissinger and the memories of several elephants! Well my father probably would have failed on the last one, so to counteract this he meticulously kept a diary of all his work activities from 1922 right through to 1965. His was a breed that I like to think helped make Great Britain the great country that it once was: selfless devotion to duty was not unusual to men of his ilk, a job well done usually the only reward. This leadership by example imbibed similar qualities in others responsible for the smooth running of the various departments within an engine shed: I have to say that perhaps the greatest thrill for me whilst researching this book was to find that, despite the passing of 40 years or more, my father's memory lives on and he is still highly regarded and respected by those men still living who worked for and with him.

Anthony J. Robinson
Whitchurch
2010

Chapter One

Apprenticeship Days at Willesden

John Eric Robinson was born in Crewe on 7th March, 1902, the second child and the eldest son of John Robinson, assistant chief electrical engineer to the London & North Western Railway (LNWR) who was responsible for all non-traction activities (electrical) on the 'Premier Line'. John Robinson was in turn the eldest son of the redoubtable (and famous) Ben Robinson.

In an illustrious railway career lasting 52 years, Ben Robinson had enjoyed the distinction of having driven the Royal train more frequently than any other man of his era. In 1893 he was in charge of 3-cylinder Compound 'Greater Britain' class 2-2-2-2 No. 2054 *Queen Empress* at the World's Columbia Exposition at Chicago (also known as the World's Fair). The locomotive, along with a pair of 42 ft LNWR carriages, ran as a 'British Special Train' from Chicago to New York. On 22nd August, 1895 he was at the controls of 'Precedent' class 2-4-0 No. 790 *Hardwicke* on its record-breaking run during the 'Race to the North'. The engine covered the 141 miles from Crewe to Carlisle in two hours six minutes, averaging 67.1 mph, a world speed record. Ben Robinson set another world record with three-cylinder Compound 'Teutonic' class 2-2-2-0 No. 1306 *Ionic* on 8th September, 1895 when the locomotive hauled a train non-stop from London (Euston) to Carlisle, a distance of 299¼ miles.

Around about 1910 the family moved from Edleston Road, Crewe to Elm Road, Wembley following a promotional move by my grandfather to the head offices at Euston.

On completion of his education at Harrow (County) School in 1919 my dad applied for an apprenticeship with Napier's, renowned for their aero engine developments during and after the 'war to end all wars'. By contemporary standards his educational background was excellent and he was offered a non-premium apprenticeship, something highly sought after in those days. However, there was a snag, a place could not be made available for him immediately and he was asked to wait for a specified period of about six months before starting (perhaps a lost opportunity to work with the late great R.J. Mitchell on the Schneider trophy seaplanes!). As he had by now left school, with no wish to return, his father pulled strings in high places (his friend and neighbour was the LNWR London area district locomotive superintendent (DLS) Francis W. Dingley) and gained him a temporary position in the LNWR workshops which were part of Willesden sheds.

Like so many things the temporary position became permanent; sentimentalists like myself might like to believe it was because that dirty old contrivance, the steam locomotive, got into his blood! The real truth I will never know, for the position at Napier's was made available in due course but he then turned it down. So he commenced an apprenticeship as a locomotive fitter with the 'Premier Line', under the disciplined stewardship of W.R. (Bill) Clements the works foreman. Fitter was probably a not very apt description as my dad was very much an engineer! Adept at mathematics and engineering drawing he

A Robinson family photograph *circa* 1892. Ben Robinson is seated second from the left in the centre row. The author's grandfather, John, is top left.   *Author's Collection*

LNWR 'Precedent' class No. 790 *Hardwicke*. An official works photograph showing Ben Robinson and his fireman Bill Wolstencroft aboard their steed after their unqualified success with the Crewe to Carlisle portion on the last night of the 'Race to the North' in August 1895.
LNWR Society

Ben Robinson poses on the footplate of 'Jubilee' class 4-4-0 No. 1926 outside the paint shop at Crewe works on 16th July, 1900. This locomotive was the 4,000th built at Crewe.

LNWR Society/E. Talbot Collection

Willesden erecting shop *circa* 1921. We see activity over the wheel drop in front of a Webb tank engine. The figure second from right is the redoubtable foreman fitter W.R. (Bill) Clements. Judging by the direction of the sunlight it was early morning. The photographer is Joe Shervington.   *LNWR Society/J.M. Dunn Collection*

Another Joe Shervington view shows the third road in the erecting shop which was not served by the overhead crane. There is an alarming jumble of eccentrics, valve rods, and assorted bits on the motion bench. The suspended extraction hood for the whitesmith's hearth can be seen in the background. The steam-driven belt and pulleys serving two lathes, a vertical drilling/boring machine, an 1847 wheel lathe, a planer, a tube cutting saw bench and a grindstone can be seen in the far background.   *LNWR Society/J.M. Dunn Collection*

studied throughout the tenure of his apprenticeship at night school. There was no day release in those days, his subject like mine was mechanical engineering, and whilst initially he was a student at Paddington Technical Institute he went on to study at Regent Street Polytechnic, finally ending up with a year at the London School of Economics. He was always very modest about his academic achievements and to this day I've never found out exactly what qualifications he gained, but judging by the standards of some of the text books that I still have, and refer to occasionally, he studied to at least the old Higher National Certificate (HNC) standard. This is some measure of his determination, as to get that far working purely on a night school basis takes some doing! To the best of my knowledge he did not actually, unlike his lifelong friend Maxwell Dunn, apply to become a Member of the Institution of Locomotive Engineers. His immediate post-apprenticeship move to North Wales in 1925 probably precluded any further advancement in that direction.

He often related stories of note and amusement from his apprenticeship days; one that particularly sticks in my mind actually happened on his very first day at Willesden. He was engaged with a number of fitters in removing the rear radial truck from one of Webb's small tank engines, when suddenly it broke loose from one of its shackles and part of it fell on his foot! His working day was somewhat curtailed and he wound up at home well before his due time. Well, that's what he told me anyhow, no doubt a visit to the surgery was fitted in there somewhere. If it had been me I would have said, 'Stick this for a game of soldiers, I'll wait until Napier's are ready for me!' But not my dad, he was back there bright and early next morning ready for his next round of punishment. So it went on right through his career: he had more split finger nails, cuts and bruises, than hot dinners, not to mention steam scalds and a serious arm slice on a copper tube plate edge! A more amusing anecdote was that of getting changed out of his working clothes whilst going up the escalator at Baker Street tube station. Apparently there were a group of night school apprentices and this was one of their not untypical tricks.

Whether my dad was a true masochist or not is open to debate but he did have an uncanny knack of sorting out locomotive troubles, and it was this mechanical empathy that was probably more responsible than anything else for tying him to the steam locomotive for the rest of his life and career. He once proudly related an incident during his days at Willesden. By 'invitation' he got involved in a valve setting problem on a non-superheated 'D' class 0-8-0 class engine. Apparently the foreman was going 'off his head' trying to get this particular engine to run. The engine had been coupled to a 'George V' class and was being desperately dragged up and down the yard in what had become a vain attempt to get its valve settings right following reassembly after a major overhaul. One can almost hear the foreman shouting at a grinning John Eric, 'Well if you think you're so bloody clever, then have a go yourself!' Which of course he did, or I wouldn't be telling this tale. He went back into the workshops whence from his tool box he extricated his valve setting trammels (perhaps prepared earlier for just such an event!). The said implements were then given a highly notable application which I am assured was a resounding success. The 'George V' was uncoupled and my dad drove the 'D' off down the yard without any further ado! Just what the human reaction was

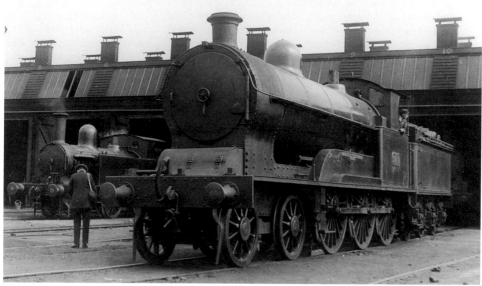

'Experiment' class 4-6-0 No. 1988 *Hurricane* at Willesden shed *circa* 1920. Another photographer can be seen recording the Webb Radial tank in the background.   *LNWR Society Collection*

A mishap at Kings Langley in September 1922. A 'Super D' 0-8-0 has run off the end of the down loop slip into the street below and attracts considerable attention from the local populace, including the press.   *J.M. Dunn Archives*

I can only guess, but as his apprenticeship was nearly over along with his studies, it may have had something to do with his swift flight to North Wales. Although to be fair he always claimed that the real reason was his desire to get out of range of his father's influence, he was a proudly independent man and was keen to avoid claims of nepotism should any positions be made available for him. Max Dunn thought he was crazy and claimed, to me at any rate, that with his family influence and training a nice position at Crewe or later maybe Derby would have been made available to him. To this day some of those old specialist tools, some of which he not only made but designed, still exist in his old tool chest. It is a great pity that nearly all of the engines they were made to fit were so mercilessly cut up by the post-Grouping London, Midland & Scottish Railway (LMS) regime.

During his apprenticeship days he made two life-long friends who were to become, along with their wives, like members of our family. The first has already been mentioned, J. Maxwell Dunn, who, although a few years older than my dad, befriended him when he first arrived at Willesden. Max was the archetypal railway enthusiast who joined the LNWR because of his sheer admiration for it, and he remained a student and worshipper of all things 'North Western' until the day he died. The second was Joe Shervington who was in turn a few years younger than dad. He was known to him from schooldays prior to joining the LNWR (in its very last year of existence), as the Shervington family lived nearby in Wembley. Joe later moved his apprenticeship at the behest of his father, to Staplefords at Coalville who were carriage and wagon builders and repairers. I will relate later the experiences that I had with these two most notable of characters, suffice to say that both had influence on both my father and myself (in my early years).

This is the earliest official photograph, taken at Euston in 1925, that the author has of his father on railway business. It is believed to be the occasion of the lunch to mark the end of his father's and his colleagues' apprenticeships. J.E. Robinson is third from the right in the back row.
Author's Collection

Ben Robinson's grandson, and the author's father, J.E. Robinson, stands in front of *Hardwicke* flanked by wife Martha and daughter Ann outside Llandudno Junction shed in July 1948. The author was present, but would not put in an appearance until the end of the year!   *J.M. Dunn*

Chapter Two

Llandudno Junction, 1925-1945

If this were a biography of my father's life and career, then almost half of it would be based on his experiences at Llandudno Junction shed, for that is where he spent the greatest number of years. His contempories (if they were still alive) would readily testify to his justifiable lack of respect for the then divisonal locomotive superintendent. It was not until the said gentleman retired that my father got his first long overdue promotion to leading fitter at Rhyl shed in 1946. True enough he had worked in a semi-supervisory capacity at Denbigh shed way back in 1932 for a short while, but this was a real and 'permanent' position made all the more available to him by the leading fitter at the Junction, a brick of a man called Tom Maclay, 'Tommy Mac' for short, but more about him later. I think at this point it is worth relating a little of my dad's background so as to give the reader some perspective to my somewhat patchy reminiscences as they unravel.

In 1925 my dad accepted a vacancy as a fitter at Llandudno Junction (7A) shed on the banks of the Conway estuary in North Wales. Whilst the 'Junction', as it was always known, came under the umbrella of the DLS at Crewe along with all the other 'A' sheds in the North West division of the LMS, it was the central and most important motive power depot on the coast. Most sheds were 'Garage' depots but the Junction was home for the DLS and housed facilities for full running repair work, featuring such equipment as a wheel drop and machine workshop. The other sheds in the division at that time were Bangor, Holyhead, Rhyl, Denbigh and Caernarvon. So having become fully versed at Willesden in the ramifications of light to medium running repairs on the different engines of the North Western stud, he set about work in the idyllic surroundings of that beautiful Conway valley estuary. He established himself in a comfortable 'digs' in Avallon Avenue at the top of 'The Hill' (the area in Llandudno Junction to the east of the station was on high ground and was generally referred to as 'up the hill'). He settled in for what became a very long spell 'on the bench'. Hours were long and the work was unremittingly hard; no stranger to this he found himself with what I believe were more than his fair share of 'dog's jobs'.

One particular regular 'treat' was the hand cutting of brass eccentric strap bearings. These arrived in the stores van from Crewe as rough castings and had to be made to fit the individual locomotive *in situ*, the only way to do this was to hand chisel out the bearing running surface on a fit and try basis. To anyone versed in mechanical fitting the job immediately conjures up nightmarish problems! Now let's move the job from the textbook manageability of the bench and vice take it down under the locomotive into a dark, slippery and dirty pit. Couple this to a job normally done on the nightshift and mix in a cold wind coming in off the estuary and blowing down the length of the shed. The wind not only chilling one to the bone but playing havoc with the stone age illumination offered by the flickering paraffin Aladdin's lamps strategically

Llandudno Junction

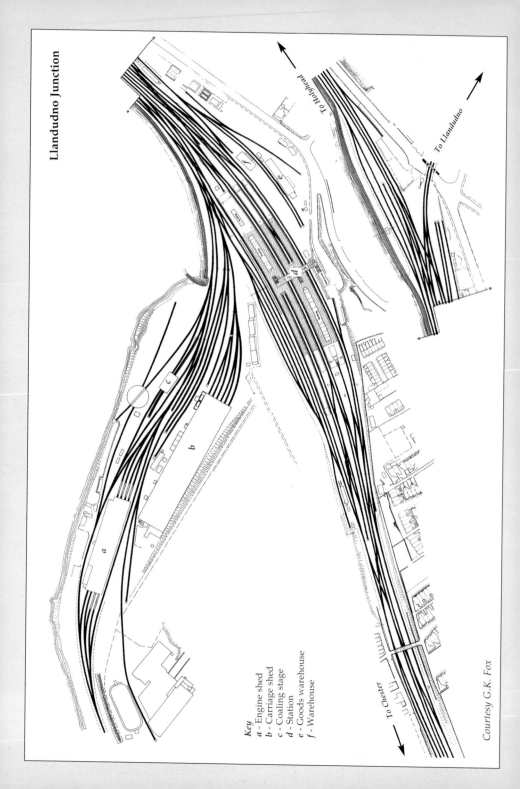

To Holyhead

To Llandudno

To Chester

Key
a - Engine shed
b - Carriage shed
c - Coaling stage
d - Station
e - Goods warehouse
f - Warehouse

Courtesy G.K. Fox

placed around the work area. I often wonder if today's steam enthusiasts really have a clue as to how difficult life was for the 'professionals' all those years ago! At this point I would like to include some notes made by my father's friend the late Maxwell Dunn, who for a period between the wars was employed at Llandudno Junction shed as fitter in charge. These words serve to exemplify some of the real difficulties that my father and his contemporaries laboured under in their efforts to keep the ex-LNWR locomotives running:

The 4 ft 3 in. 0-6-2 side tank coal engines may be taken as fairly representative of the small engines, all the tank variety of which with the exception of the saddle tanks had the tank filling aperture in the coal bunker conveniently placed so as to receive any coal that might be displaced by a man standing on top of the coal while attending to the filling of the tanks by the water column bag. In course of time coal rails were fitted round the bunker to increase the coal capacity and an extension about 12 to 18 inches high was fitted over the tank aperture to raise the level of the lid. This meant that anyone having to get into the bunker tank to clean it etc. had to descend through about 2 feet of chimney, an exceedingly uncomfortable adventure. This had to be done fairly frequently as the coal having got into the tank would break-up, get past the tank feed valves in spite of their being fitted with brass sieves rather like inverted colanders and so into the injectors. The latter were of three sizes viz. 9 mm, 10 mm and 11 mm. The injectors would not inject due to bits of coal etc. in the cones or under the clack valve. The injectors could not be dismantled in position - they were screwed on to the lower end of a vertical stand pipe called the barrel at the top of which was a three-winged clack valve and seating, the whole contraption being between 4 and 5 feet long and fixed vertically between the firebox back plate and the footplate casting. The union nut attaching the steam pipe to the injector, the feed pipe nut and the nut at the top of the barrel by which the clack and its seating were coupled to the clack box all had to be unscrewed before the contrivance could be lowered. The steam pipe nut was almost out of sight and could only be reached with a claw-foot spanner but the feed pipe nut was not much trouble. The clack box nut, however, was a real tartar although in full sight and easy reach on the footplate. A horse-shoe spanner was the only sort that would go anywhere near it and then only by prizing the adjacent steam pipe and ram rod clear. As soon as the two latter were released they would immediately push the spanner off the nut so that more often than not it would be loosened by blows from a hand hammer. Of course a spanner had to be used to lighten it which was a two-man job.

To get at the clack the whole lot had to be lowered about six inches which was bad enough but to attend to the injector cones all the 4 or 5 feet of misery had to be taken right down, removed to a bench and put in a vice so that it could be dismantled. In the case of the big boilered engines the barrel would be so long that it had to be disconnected from the injector in the pit under the engine which was another unavoidable struggle. Sometimes on these big engines the injector fitted so snugly between the footplate and the boiler door plate that it had to be prised up inch by inch with a heavy pinch bar manipulated on the footplate.

The injector clack box I have mentioned was fitted with a stop valve between the clack and the injector delivery pipe which put the cold water into the boiler at a point about half way between the dome and the smokebox tubeplate. The stop valve had a nasty habit of suddenly starting to blow along its screw thread and spurt steam and hot water across the footplate. It was usually fatal to move the stop valve wheel unless to close it against the delivery pipe and attempts to open it still wider and so tighten the threads to stop the blow generally made bad worse. Once in an emergency in an endeavour to avoid a delay to an important train I tried to change one of these valves without putting out the fire. I knew from experience that if the water level in the boiler was only just

Llandudno Junction shed *circa* 1930. Just two engines can be seen in this rather dull view, a Webb tank plus the rear view of what is probably a 4-4-0 'George V' class. Note the DLS's office bay window to the right of the shed entrance. Behind this were further offices plus the main machine and fitting shops. An interesting train of wagons stands on the siding to the left, the rear part of which appears to be empties awaiting shunting into the adjacent brickworks.

J.M. Dunn

above the bottom nut of the gauge glass, a few seconds elapsed after taking out the stop valve before the water began to flow out, so I decided that if I had everything ready and was quick enough I might manage to put in a new valve. I therefore smothered the low fire with small coal, blew out all the steam and removed the defective valve easily enough. I managed to insert the new valve but unfortunately got it cross-threaded so that I could not screw it home before the hot water came back and scalded the fingers of my right hand very badly. I am sorry to say I forget what happened to the engine and its train but there is no doubt that in my undoubtedly misplaced enthusiasm I acted very foolishly and should never have made the attempt.

Due to the standard of technical education that my father received during his apprenticeship it frequently fell to his lot to do the more highly technical jobs which involved preparing drawings and reports. As there were no facilities at the shed he invariably did this sort of work at home in his own time. I still have the old drawing board and T-square which he later used when a shed master for preparing engine/crew working diagrams (*see Chapter Six*).

Being very much an Englishman, he was a 'Foreigner' to the other lads in the shed and to this end he very quickly earned the nickname of 'Wembley'. They almost to a man spoke Welsh fluently and when it was discovered that he had befriended the local curate, he was a devout churchman all his life, they set about 'teaching' him some of their hallowed tongue! It went without saying that the curate would be Welsh speaking also and no doubt would be somewhat impressed if his learned English friend was able to engage him with a profound 'well known phrase or saying', and so it came to pass ... the phrase turned out to be a question which began with the words 'Syd mae di ...?' The rest of it referred to a part of the male anatomy which shall remain within the reader's imagination! Happily the curate was a young man who, like my father, possessed a wicked sense of humour; when he made the translation he adjoined it with a suitable riposte in the mother tongue and instructed dad to repeat it in due course to the wags at the shed! Time has erased the details but one can surmise as to what the phraseology amounted to.

Just across the road from the Junction station was, and is still extant, a small shop on the corner of Conway Road and Broad Street. Shoe-horned twixt a larger grocer shop and a high wall adjoining the said street, it was built of timber and in the mid-twenties served as a combined gents' barber and sweet/tobacconist's shop. I think dad had smoked a pipe since they invented the word, needless to say such a vice needed a 'coaling stage' and this small almost insignificant edifice, situated as it was, proved to be just what the doctor ordered. Not only could he replenish his tobacco pouch but get his ears lowered as and when it became necessary! This small business was owned by a certain ex-Royal Welch Fusilier named Harry Davies and his wife Margaret. Sadly Harry, who before the war had been an up and coming landscape gardener in and around the Junction, had been badly injured in a bomb blast at Paschendale. As he was now severely disabled and confined to a bath chair, he resolved to take care of his family's welfare by opening the aforementioned shop. Bravely, despite great pain and discomfort from his wounds, he manned the shop daily, his eldest daughter Martha assisting him as soon as she left school. He leased out the section at the rear of the shop to a local barber. After

Page 1

Marriage solemnized at St Michael's Church in the Parish of Llangyolenni in the County of Caernarvon

1922.

No.	When Married.	Name and Surname.	Age.	Condition.	Rank or Profession.	Residence at the time of Marriage.	Father's Name and Surname.	Rank or Profession of Father.
1	May 16th 1932	John Eric Robinson	30	Bachelor	Fitter	5 Avallon Ao Penmaenmawr	John Robinson Sn.	Electrical Engineer
		Martha Davies	23	Spinster	—	5 Maelgwr Llandudno Jn.	Harry Pewter Davies	Garden Sec.

Married in the Church according to the Rites and Ceremonies of the Church in Wales by ____ or after Banns by me,

This Marriage was solemnized between us, } John Eric Robinson, Martha Davies } in the Presence of us, } J. T. Williams Rector

Marriage solemnized at St Michael's Church in the Parish of Llangyolenni in the County of Caernarvon.

1932.

No.	When Married.	Name and Surname.	Age.	Condition.	Rank or Profession.	Residence at the time of Marriage.	Father's Name and Surname.	Rank or Profession of Father.
2	September 17th 1932	Walter Thomas	27	Bachelor	Gardener	19 High Street Penmaenmawr	Richard Thomas	Ferryman
		Elizabeth Johnson	24	Spinster	—	12 Stanparks Rd Llandudno Junction	Thomas Johnson	Gas works foreman

Married in the Church of St Michael according to the Rites and Ceremonies of the Church in Wales by ____ or after Banns by me,

This Marriage was solemnized between us, } Elizabeth Johnson, Walter Thomas } in the Presence of us, } Agnes Mary Childs } J. T. Williams Rector

Any Correctional Notes must be written in this margin.

The marriage certificate, from St Michael's church, Llandudno Junction. On the sad occasion of my mother's funeral in October 1999 I was given access to the first wedding register of the church which shows the first ever entry to be 16th May, 1932 - John Robinson and Martha Davies. My mother supported the church throughout her life. Upon my father's death in 1967 she presented the church with a silver altar cross and a set of matching candlestick holders in his memory.

Author

a long and harrowing illness which meant that his personal input in the shop became more and more curtailed, Harry died at the tragically early age of thirty-nine. This left Martha in sole charge of the shop, as her mother had to work elsewhere as a cook to earn sufficient income to feed and house the family which comprised also of Martha's younger brother Norman and sister Sophie; the year was 1925.

Well time went on and needless to say Martha got on famously with the well-spoken young fitter from the shed and soon a friendship started to develop. Martha quickly realised that steam locomotives were the enduring passion of his life and decided that if she were to maintain his ongoing interest, then conversation needed to be spiced up with the odd 'key' word. One of her mother's brothers just happened to be a driver at the Junction shed, his name was Lewis Evans and he was a man of some experience, especially on the Blaenau Ffestiniog branch. Lewis ruefully realising the delicateness of the situation, and knowing that a little knowledge is a dangerous thing, must have decided that if he gave her enough rope she would hang herself! So armed with insider names such as 'Caprotti, Tishy, Joy's etc.' she attempted to spark up a discussion on the merits of different valve gear. Her suitor realised that she had been set up and took a not uninspired guess as to who the culprit was!

After a not untypically long courtship, for the period, they married at St Michael's church, Llandudno Junction in May 1932. My mother took great pride in the fact that their names were the first to appear in the register of what was a brand new church (building). After a honeymoon with friends at Sidmouth on the East Devon coast they returned to the Junction and life quickly settled down to a routine with my father working alternate months of night and day shifts at the shed. The overbearing memory that my mother has of those early days was of 'always waiting for your father to come home ...' Sure enough it was either because of a problem breaking out at the end of shift time or, as was frequently the case, a breakdown. Dad had always been a member of the breakdown gang wherever he had worked. As a fitter it was a means of earning a little bit of overtime for out of hours work and later as a 'Gaffer' it was part and parcel of the job.

I don't have too many recollections of his stories of pre-war breakdowns save for one which he told me about whilst we were riding in the front compartment of a 'Derby Lightweight' diesel-multiple-unit (dmu) to Blaenau Ffestiniog one morning in October 1958.

We had not long left Bettws-y-Coed and were climbing the bank on Gethins Bridge viaduct when he suddenly blurted out, 'The last time I was here it was to put a Fowler ['4F' class] back on the road!' It then transpired that once upon a time, fortunately on a bright and sunny day, back in the 1930s a Fowler '4F' had for some reason been substituted for the usual LNWR 'Cauliflower' on the daily pick-up goods to Blaenaue Ffestiniog . Everything had gone well until the esteemed engine had reached a bend on the up side of Gethins Bridge when suddenly she split the road and rolled forth on the sleepers! Providence decreed that the driver was able to stop her before she rolled off the track bed and down a steep gorge into the rocky River Lledr below. One can only surmise that either the track bend was a tad too sharp or maybe gauged a weenie bit too narrowly

Captured at its home shed, Llandudno Junction in 1933 is ex-LNWR 'Claughton' class 4-6-0 No. 5991 *C.J. Bowen Cooke*. Having something of a reputation with valve setting my dad regularly had the job of keeping this four-cylinder beauty 'in tune' along with some of the more mundane tasks that befell the fitters' lot. Crewe kept this engine in its original black livery until 1928 before progress dictated it be turned out in LMS red. The engine was sadly turned into 'mechanical mincemeat' in February 1935. The photographer, Harry Hall, rescued the chimney and one of the nameplates shown here. What a candidate for presevation it would have been!

Harry Hall/J.M. Bentley Collection

August 1934, and No. 5991 is seen backing onto its train at the up end of Llandudno Junction station. This locomotive was something of an LNWR icon, being named after its designer and built in the month of his death, October 1920. At the time it was the cream of the shed's allocation and diagrammed in summer months to work the 'Welshman', in winter it regularly worked the 'Manchester Club'. From 1909 until 1923 'The Welshman' made the longest regular non-stop run on the LNWR. The train left Euston at 11.15 am and ran non-stop to Rhyl (209.1 miles). Normally the train was divided at Rhyl, with the restaurant car portion arriving at Llandudno at 4.02 pm and the last portion arriving at Pwllheli at 5.45 pm. By 1934 the up train portions left Portmadoc at 9.35 am, and Pwllheli 9.50 am and joined the Llandudno portion at Llandudno Junction at 11.44 am.

Harry Hall/J.M. Bentley Collection

Llandudno Junction examinations, washout and repairs board in 1936.

J.M. Dunn/LNWR Society

Caerwys (Mold & Denbigh line) in April 1936. A sheared rear driving axle renders ex-LNWR 'George V' class 4-4-0 No. 5343 *Otterhound* a 'failure'. It is seen here being lifted by Chester's steam crane so that the offending rear axle and wheels can be removed prior to re-wheeling and dragging back to Llandudno Junction shed for full reports. *J.M. Dunn*

In June 1937 the LMS launched a publicity campaign for the new blue streamlined 'Coronation Scot'. Ex-Liverpool & Manchester Railway 0-4-2 *Lion* with a vintage train stands alongside the Stanier Pacific at Llandudno Junction prior to the two trains running alongside each other to Colwyn Bay.   *J.M. Dunn*

Lion and the vintage train back over the turntable at Llandudno Junction. The streamlined Stanier Pacific can be seen to the left in the far distance.   *J.M. Dunn*

The nameplate from 'Claughton' class 4-4-0 No. 5991 *C.J. Bowen Cooke*.   *Author*

for the relatively 'stiff' chassis of the Fowler, either way I don't think the class was used again on the branch.(No doubt somebody out there will produce a photograph to prove me wrong!) I don't recall the method of re-railing that was employed but no doubt given the narrow and dangerous location it was a somewhat precarious operation.

I remember in the mid-1950s when the 'powers that be' decreed that all London Midland Region shed masters and divisional motive power superintendents (DMPS) were to go on familiarization courses for diesel locomotives. These courses were generally held at the staff training college at Derby. Dad came home muttering that, 'Those infernal things will fail if so much as a fuse blows!' Of course he then went on to relate how back in the 1930s a Junction driver had nursed a 'Claughton' home with half of its outside motion missing. It appears that for whatever reason the locomotive concerned had 'thrown' its return crank and eccentric rod on the left (driver's) side, with obvious catastrophic results for the remaining valve gear on that side. However, on coming to a stop the driver and fireman had managed to remove the 'dangly bits' and, stowing them in the tender, had managed to restart the engine and nurse it home to the shed! I cannot recollect whether the engine was uncoupled from its train or not.

Another story which my father often liked to relate was again about something that had happened in the 1930s. It concerned the up 'Irish Mail', the motive power involved was I think a modified (large boilered) 'Claughton'. Apparently the signalman at Penmaenmawr had called Control at the Junction to say that the train was going to have to make an unscheduled stop to have some urgent 'quick' on the spot repair or adjustment work done and could a fitter be ready at the station when the train arrived? Again time has erased exactly what the problem was suffice to say it was at the front end of the engine and therefore probably something to do with a valve rod or gland.* Well the train limped in and our man was there with his mobile tool kit, a Gladstone bag full of tools. I think it took about 30 minutes but the job was done and off went the 'flagship train' leaving one relieved but satisfied fitter standing on the platform!

---

* These four-cylinder locomotives had an 'Achilles' heel' in that the settings on the inside valves suffered from heat expansion of the outside valve rods which drove them through pivoted lever arms. This expansion then effected the events of the inside cylinder's valves in relation to the outside cylinder's valves.

The up 'Irish Mail' *circa* 1930s enters Llandudno Junction station behind un-named 'Claughton' class 4-6-0 No. 5994.
Harry Hall/J.M. Bentley Collection

Llandudno Junction's breakdown crane with the breakdown van at Bangor *circa* 1953.
J.M. Dunn/LNWR Society

Chapter Three

Wartime

Being born in 1902 my father was too old at 37 to be called up for service in the armed forces, also it could be argued that his job would have given him special dispensation. When one considers the state the railways got into over the years of the 'Duration' it would come as no surprise that the fitters' lot was not a happy one! With locomotive production at Crewe and Derby ceasing altogether in favour of armament manufacture, and locomotive heavy repairs being put off until deemed absolutely necessary, the strain on the sheds would become almost intolerable by 1945. One of the first things that my father and many of his colleagues got involved in during their spare time was the St John's Ambulance Brigade which had a headquarters at Llandudno. At the outbreak of hostilities it was LMS dictum that first aid training was undertaken by key members of all departments (usually volunteers). My mother had in her possession various medals and diplomas that he gained during his fairly long voluntary service with the local St John's Brigade. I also know that in subsequent years he frequently put into good effect his knowledge of first aid as all too often a loco shed is the scene of injury, sometimes serious. (It's surprising even today in industry just how few people are trained in the basic rudiments of essential first aid.) Engine sheds always have been very dangerous places for those uninitiated in the basic rules of railway safety. However, I digress, it was expected that even backwaters such as the North Wales coast would be targets for Teutonic aggression, so all thoughts were put into means of averting or at least minimizing potential disasters.

With the horrors of World War I still fresh in the minds of many, it was presumed that one of Hitler's main weapons would be the use of phosgene or 'Mustard' gas, deployed in all probability during air raids. Moving trains were considered to be prime potential targets, in consequence of this my father set about producing plans for dealing with the gas hazard should it be encountered on trains on the Chester-Holyhead line. At the rear of the Junction shed the through and shed by-pass roads tapered off to the truncated spur of the old route of the Blaenau Ffestiniog branch. This old branch line was by now only used for the storage of disused locomotives and coal wagons, etc. It ran for about a half mile alongside the Conway river estuary before ending at a stop block some 200 yards short of the new branch line formation. He produced drawings and plans for the rapid sea water washing of trains which, should they be gas-bombed, as quickly as possible would be shunted down this old line formation and spray washed with water under high pressure from the adjacent tidal river. History would relate that fortunately such drastic measures never became necessary, but somehow I wonder about the practicality or indeed the better alternatives to such a scheme as mooted. Carriages in those days were hardly hermetically sealed and for those unfortunates within who had 'forgotten' their Government issue gas masks, the horror of being 'entombed' in a train drenched in liquid gas does not bear thinking about. Similar 'gas washing' facilities were also proposed for

Holyhead. That neither system was adopted probably had as much to do with the fact that the fearsome medium was never adopted by the enemy as it had to do with the practical problems of its effective implementation. Having said that, no better solutions to the perceived threat had been proposed by any other parties to the best of my knowledge.

A regular voluntary service performed by my father and many of the other shed staff was that of 'fire watching'. This was performed on a rotational basis nightly throughout the war, Deganwy Quay being the venue for dad's stints. This was a large wooden dock built by the LNWR for the transhipping from rail to ship of the expected slate traffic from the Ffestiniog quarries. The quay had been equipped with four standard gauge sidings and adjacent 2 ft gauge tracks for the movement of the narrow gauge tubs or trucks which would have been brought down from the quarries on the backs of special standard gauge 'transporter' wagons via the Blaenau Ffestiniog branch. The quay was situated on the opposite bank of the river from Conway alongside the double track Llandudno branch. By the time war broke out it had fallen out of its original use as the slate traffic had never reached the expected volume, thanks to such competing enterprises as the Great Western Railway (GWR) (standard gauge) and the Festiniog Railway (2 ft gauge), so the LMS used it for the winter stabling of coaching stock.

Many cold winter nights were spent fruitlessly listening to and watching the German bombers above grinding their way towards Liverpool laden with their deadly cargoes, then would come the remorseless 'bump-crump' as they unloaded just 40 miles away. It was said by the locals that moonlight nights were welcomed by the bomber crews who used the mouth of the River Conway to take a final directional heading towards their Mersey goal. One night a lone bomber returning from a raid unloaded a single 'egg' onto the side of Conway Mountain, just near to where the Morfa gasworks once stood. This time the people of Llandudno had just cause to take cover when the air raid sirens sounded: that single bomb took out nearly every unprotected pane of glass in the town, such was the reflected blast effect off the mountainside! To my knowledge no further 'air raids' were made on the immediate area, although my dad once remarked, 'If Jerry had dropped bombs on the south side of Snowdon, he would have blown up half of North Wales!' By that I assumed he meant that there were large amounts of munitions and fuel stored in the mountains and adjoining valleys.

My father's parents, the late John Robinson and his wife, had moved from Wembley to Margate on the Kent coast on his retirement from the LMS in the early 1930s. All students of war history will recall that the end of the Kent peninsula became known as 'Hell Fire Corner' due to the ferocious air 'dog fights' that went on in the skies over the Isle of Thanet area during the 'Battle of Britain' in 1940. My grandparents were quick to realise the danger of remaining in the area and a rapid evacuation ensued. A small rented house in Glan Conway was selected as the 'Robbo's residence' and that is where John Robinson, late assistant chief electrical engineer of the LNWR/LMS lived out his final years. It always seemed to me that my father was very much in awe of his own father, who it has to be said was very 'Victorian' in his approach to life. When before war broke out *mon père* consulted him on buying one of a small number of 'three up, two down' semi-detached houses that were nearing completion at the top of 'the hill' in Llandudno Junction, he was firmly rebuked with negative advice over borrowing money (via a mortgage, then about 15s. a month). This 'advice' was further augmented by my grandfather who opined that the houses were of poor quality and not worth the asking price! So our family continued to live in council houses paying 'dead' rent until 1963, when my father had saved up enough money to almost purchase a house outright - bad advice indeed. His father was never to return to his neat 'semi' in Margate, for he soon developed a serious illness (prostate cancer) from which he did not recover. He died in February 1944 and was buried in the parish churchyard of Llangystenin near Mochdre.

One of the enduring features of my father's lifestyle was his penchant for keeping a diary. At one time in the drawer at the bottom of his desk bureau was kept a collection of personal pocket diaries dating from 1922 to 1965! Unfortunately, some years after I married and left home my mother somewhat misguidedly disposed of them. Fortunately, I was able to find just one which had escaped the refuse collectors' attentions, it is a leather bound official LMS diary for 1943. The front cover bears the company crest and within it are to be found some interesting facts and figures about the railway company as at the period prior to the outbreak of war. Many of the details are well known to students of LMS history but there are a few items that I think are less well known, below are some details listed as statistics for 1938:

No. of stockholders	319,600
No. of staff employed	233,000
Salaries and wages paid	£41,434,600
(averages out at £3 8s. 2½d. per week)	
No. of locomotives	7,644
No. of passenger carrying vehicles.	17,478
With seating capacity	1,068,800
No. of merchandise / min. vehicles	279,994
With tonnage capacity of	3,284,144
No. of steamboats	43
No. of horses	7,475
No. of road vehicles for horses	16,629
No. of road motors for cartage	3,454
Coal consumed by steam locomotives (tons)	5,500,325
Passenger traffic receipts	£27,076,728
Goods traffic receipts	£36,485,663

There is no record of the tonnage of equine manure generated!

Another page gives authenticated speeds achieved by some LMS locomotives as follows:

Type	Class	Coupled wheels	Speed (mph)
4-cylinder 4-6-2	7	6 ft 9 in.	114.4
'Royal Scot'	6	6 ft 9 in.	92
3-cylinder 4-6-0	5X	6 ft 9 in.	91
2-cylinder 4-6-0	5	6 ft 0 in.	91
Compound	4	6 ft 9 in.	87

It's interesting to see the compound in there at 87 mph, I'll bet the ride at that speed was lively to say the least!

The two largest signal boxes are listed as Glasgow Central with 374 levers (power-operated), followed by Euston No. 2 with 288 manually-operated levers.

The contents of the diary follow very much the same lines as the preceding and subsequent versions. Each day's work activities are logged in almost intricate detail together with a brief mention of anything special that may have happened at home. He once admitted to me that he logged his work details because of an inherently poor memory for detail, something I've also inherited! I've listed a few entries that may be of interest to those who have a fascination for the working routine of shed life.

Two typical days (remember the year is 1943) …

Tuesday March 23rd
6.00 am-6.30 pm D1086, 936, 7802. X1118, 5052-bearings various. 1119 cyls tested with water & leak under lower steam chest.

Thursday March 25th
6.00 am-3.30 pm D1098, 8552, 4389, 7802, 1118, 1086, 413 & bearings. Sketching cracked frame 3877.

Days when something 'non routine' happened:

Wednesday April 14th
Repaired hosepipe for ashpit.

Wednesday July 21st
ARP lecture at station.

Saturday August 14th
Breakdown at Caernarvon.

Tuesday August 24th
An American 2-8-0 on shed.

Wednesday September 8th
ITALY SURRENDERED. (In capitals!)

Chapter Four

Post-War Progress

From about the end of March of that year he seems to have been promoted to chargehand fitter, whether this was permanent or not is difficult to tell as it is written as a heading on certain days only to begin with and then it appears just about every day! Another regular occurrence is the duty of turntable oiling and greasing, this seems to take place at least once a week, although I guess the duty was a shared one amongst the fitters. The hours worked follow a pattern of three days of 6.00 am to 6.30 pm followed by two days of 6.00 am to 3.30 pm. Long hours for so little pay! Oh yes, that is in there too, the weekly pay varied between a low of £3 15s. 5d. to the 'film star' rate of £7 9s. 6d. One can only surmise that the latter was for an exorbitantly long and hard week!

One of the books that my dad kept on his shelf in his days as a shedmaster was *Locomotive Running Shed Management* by Paterson & Webster. Within are to be found several handwritten notes of interest, one particular note concerns the source of coal used by Llandudno Junction shed for its diagrammed workings:

Grade	Colliery	Job
1	Dalton Main/Barnboro'	Royal Scots (Holyhead)
2	Llay Main	7.48 am Club
3	Point of Ayr/Black Park	Others

If we try to analyse these notes the first thing that shows up is the general high regard for Yorkshire coal, that being designated as grade 1 and suitable for express passenger working. The Wrexham area coal follows as grade 2 and suitable for the Junction's top daily rostering for the 'Club' (*see page 37*). Clearly the sea coal comes way down the list for 'steamability' along with the coal from the erstwhile Chirk pit.

Strangely these notes are at odds with another handwritten entry to be found elsewhere in the book: 'Engines on long runs can burn more inferior coal than those that are frequently stopping, as when the action of the blast ceases, fires of poor coal go "dead" and so cause accumulation of dead ashes'. Years later he was to experience the undesirable effects of using 'hard' Yorkshire coals and their associated firing methods on engines designed to burn 'soft' Welsh coals, however, more about that anon.

There are two areas of the Junction's track layout that stand out in my memory as having their own names. They come to mind as there seems to be a disparity with the names given to them in some modern texts and photographic works and the names afforded by my father. The first refers to a small quay laid adjacent to and on the down side of the embankment known as Conway Bank which carried the main line into the castellated entrance of the Conway bridge. In a number of publications I have seen it referred to as the 'New York Siding', however, my father always called it the 'Klondyke'. The former name to the best of my knowledge was given to the long carriage siding on the up side of the main line which ran the length of Conway Cob.

I mentioned earlier that when dad commenced his tenure at the 'Junction' it was to be for a very long spell 'at the bench'. Well the popularly held belief amongst the other members of our family and friends both alive and deceased was that he made the great error of showing the boss up to be not quite the expert in locomotive affairs that he thought he was. That 'boss' was the DLS for not only the Junction shed but Rhyl, Denbigh, Bangor and Holyhead sheds. Max Dunn refers to him in his book *Reflections on a Railway Career* as Mr P. He was actually a Mr J.T. King, renowned for his all consuming desire to 'please' Crewe and all things 'above'! He had despite his relatively high office a seemingly strong sense of insecurity, and when well educated individuals such as Max or my father came along he was highly suspicious of their knowledge as insubordinates. So it would have appeared that any excuse was good enough to keep them and their likes in their places. It was not until the said gentleman retired at the end of the war that dad got his chance. As mentioned earlier the foreman fitter was a man named Tom Maclay who had been offered the chance to take on the job of leading fitter at Rhyl shed. He was a great ally of my father's and felt strongly about the way he had been treated by King. So he effectively gave up his chance of promotion in favour of my father who eagerly seized the opportunity of a command.

This group photograph shows J.T. King, R.F. Tucker and L. Williams posing in front of *Lion* when it visited Llandudno Junction in June 1937.   *J.M. Dunn*

Chapter Five

The Interim Posts

Rhyl 1945-1948

I have very little in the way of mementos of the time my father spent at Rhyl shed save for a couple of photos taken in 1947 by his friend Max. In any case the time he spent there was very short by contemporary standards. With Rhyl being very much a sub-shed of the Junction, he had on several occasions in the past worked at that depot, either as a relief fitter or deputized for the resident leading fitter who was in all but name the shed master. The shed, adjacent to the up tracks of the main line just to the west of the station, was a small building of just three roads with a 60 ft turntable tucked around the north side. Its main *raison d'etre* was to service the Vale of Clwyd branch and provide motive power for the many local passenger workings along the coast twixt Llandudno and Chester in the busy summer seasons.

One particular experience that he related about his sojourn at Rhyl sticks in my mind. It would be on very rare and 'unofficial' occasions indeed that a fitter ever got the chance to drive an engine on the main line. Dad got such a chance late one afternoon when he was about to book off and return home to the Junction. One of the Junction's Midland Compounds had arrived with a train from Manchester bound for Llandudno. The driver had got a message sent on ahead to Rhyl shed that he was having problems with the regulator valve, basically requesting some assistance if at all possible. As this train was to be my dad's transport home it was opportune that he travelled on the footplate to see if he could solve the problem or at least highlight the cause; actually he was invited to drive! Now Compounds had a peculiar double regulator valve which allowed high pressure direct steam admission to the low pressure cylinders on half to full regulator. Whilst I don't recall the exact details of the problem it's my guess that it was either sticking or not opening correctly. Anyway whether he was able to cure it is not recorded but what is notable is that he thoroughly enjoyed the stint and made up time on the climb to Llysfaen tunnel!

Another of the few events that I do recall my father telling me about connected with that shed was a breakdown that he attended in a somewhat unusual place. It concerned a loaded 15 ton mineral wagon that had gone 'on the floor' at some point near the quarry end of the branch that ran up to St George's Quarry from Foryd Junction. This event was only recalled when, back in the 1950s whilst travelling by car along the A55 near Abergele, we bumped over the then still extant level crossing near to the quarry. (A sure case of memory jogging!) A further item of interest was the mention of a daily Rhyl shed locomotive and crew roster involving a passenger train that departed from Rhyl at about 7.00 pm and ran to Whitchurch, obviously a local working that actually started at Rhyl. I think the Tattenhall-Whitchurch line lies forgotten in most people's minds but it was by all accounts a difficult route to work for freight crews in view of the ruling grades either side of Broxton. Recently a

Rhyl shed staff in November 1947. *Back row, from left to right*: T. Williams, F. Tasker, T. Austin, Bill Neal. *Middle row, left to right*, Percy Harrison, J.E. Robinson, J. Pasonage, J. McDonald, Lew Jones, Harry Boulter, Bob Jones, Percy Jones. *Front row, left to right*: ? Maddox, T. Hornby, Jack Passey, T. Molloy.   *J.M. Dunn*

My father seen here chatting to a driver at the entrance to the roofless shed. Post-war the LMS renewed the old LNWR roofs of many of the sheds on the system. Rhyl received its new concrete appendage shortly after Mold Junction.   *J.M. Dunn*

Left: J.E. (Jack) Robinson at Rhyl shed in June 1947.

J.M. Dunn

Below left & below: Dad's drawing of the Midland Compound double regulator valve and diagrammatic cylinder layout drawing, all made for the mutual improvement classes. The initial opening position allows steam to directly enter the two low pressure cylinders as well as the main high pressure cylinder, and when the valve is opened beyond the halfway point compounding starts to take place, with the steam then entering just the high pressure cylinder which then exhausts into the twin low pressure cylinders via the low pressure receiver. It was whilst dad was at Rhyl shed that he received a message requesting assistance from the driver of a Manchester-Llandudno passenger train who was having difficulties with this valve. As the locomotive in question was to provide motive power for my dad's train home he travelled on the footplate and was invited to drive. He thoroughly enjoyed his stint at the controls and made up some lost time.

Author's Collection

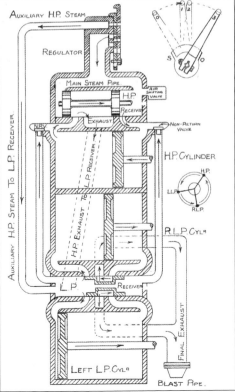

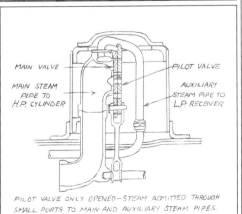

PILOT VALVE ONLY OPENED – STEAM ADMITTED THROUGH SMALL PORTS TO MAIN AND AUXILIARY STEAM PIPES.

LMS Compound No. 1115 on Crewe North shed on 26th October, 1947, with the original coaling plant and water tank in the background.   *Don Rowland*

Rhyl shed's Fowler '2P' class 4-4-0 No. 40671 backs out of the Mold bay at Chester after bringing in a Denbigh train in 1953.   *M. Baker*

colleague knowing my interest in railways approached me with the words, 'You'll never believe it but there used to be a station on the site of the picnic park at Broxton etc.' Ho, hum! Not generally known is the concept of the line put forward by G.P. Neele, the one time LNWR superintendent of the line, who in his *Railway Reminiscences* of 1904 described it as, 'a direct line of our own from Ireland to Hereford and South Wales'.*

After dad's career had lain moribund at the Junction for so many years it was understandable that he was keen to get on the promotional ladder, and so early in 1948 he applied successfully for the position of shedmaster at Sowerby Bridge. So for the first time in his career he was to leave the 'home territory' of the North Western and move to the neighbouring 'Lanc & York', as he and his peers always called it.

Sowerby Bridge 1948-1952

My enthusiasm for steam engines must have begun around about the time that I first realised that I could differentiate between a Midland Compound and a Stanier class '5', for surely it would be either one of these classes that would bring in the train that my sister and I would meet my father off on his return home every Friday evening from Yorkshire. The period would be the late summer of 1951 and the place would be platform 3 or 4 of Llandudno Junction station. At the time we lived at 13 St David's Avenue, which was a rather unimposing tree-lined road of semi-detached council houses a mere quarter of a mile from the station. My father's working week began very early each Monday morning when he would dash out of the house replete with his small suitcase to catch the the 'Manchester Club', for that was what the train continued to be known as despite the fact that officially both its name and status had died some 30 years previously along with the LNWR. On arrival at Manchester Victoria/Exchange he would board a connection bound ultimately for Halifax and Bradford, alighting at Sowerby Bridge. From the station he would proceed, no doubt somewhat nervously, to his charge … Sowerby Bridge motive power depot!

To make up for his weekday absence in Yorkshire during those early years of my life, fine Sunday mornings were invariably spent walking around the likes of Conway and its very pleasant environs. As my legs became accustomed to it, I was 'dragged' up Conway Mountain from whose lofty heights we could view the trains below running like finescale models in and out of Penmaenbach tunnel. I also remember that during summer weekends when walking along the Marine Walk at Conway, one could view across the river estuary 'trains' of light engines, often as many as four or five coupled together, returning down the Llandudno branch to the Junction shed after having brought in excursions from all over the country. It was not uncommon to see perhaps a couple of class '5s', a 'Baby Scot/Patriot', a Compound and a '5X Jubilee' in single formation.

---

* An article written by the author on the Chester-Whitchurch line appeared in the March 2007 issue of *Backtrack*.

I think that in all his 47 years of railway service the 4½ years spent at this dismal ex-Lancashire & Yorkshire Railway (L&Y) Pennine outpost were his most miserable. Indeed if one believes my mother, yours truly came to be because he was so glad to get back to the Junction at weekends! I personally have no axe to grind with the 'Yorkshire temperament', but to my father, who was a fair-minded man, who it must be said did not suffer fools gladly, the business of man management came harder at this shed than at any other place he had worked in previously or since. Maybe it was the fact that he was an old LNWR man or maybe it was just a 'pig-headed' attitude towards a stranger that did it, but the chance of a move was high on his list of priorities. There were, however, some pleasant sides to his sojourn in that steep-sided Yorkshire dale. Firstly he had an excellent landlady in Mrs Taylor: she had a delightful way with words; one particular name springs to mind, she called a bread van 'T'bun wagon'! Also to go with that her cuisine was excellent, this was vouched for by both my mother and sister who once went over to stay for a long weekend. My father was a lover of the countryside and on fine summer evenings would enjoy walking over the hills to such places as the neighbouring village of Triangle. It's fair to say that the 4½ years spent at this depot did something to enhance his respect for L&Y engines if not for the men. For example an Aspinall came out of it several points ahead of a Webb in the league table of what one today would call 'operator friendly'! He had a particular fondness for the Radial 2-4-2 tank engines of that noted designer.

Sowerby Bridge motive power depot in the 1950s. Locomotives on view include ex-LMS and ex-L&YR types as well as a 'WD' Austerity 2-8-0. The six-road shed was to the north of the main line to Manchester and west of Sowerby Bridge station. The depot had a substantial coaling stage with a water tank mounted above it (*left*). The turntable is to the right of the engine shed. The shed itself was re-roofed in 1953, after dad's time there and the depot closed on 4th January, 1964.   *P. Ward/Stephenson Locomotive Society*

Chapter Six

Some Matters of Technical Interest

I mentioned earlier that one of the 'unofficial' duties that often fell to my father's lot was that of making drawings of failed components or more interestingly sketches and drawings of ideas or improvements to existing components. As an engineer I know from experience that a little knowledge can be a dangerous thing and so when dealing with matters concerning locomotives, a subject on which I possess no working experience whatsoever, I will refrain from trying to pass any judgments and stick to just reporting my reminiscences and paper discoveries (i.e. that which have lain in't bottom drawer for more years than I care to count).

A good place to start would be to mention the tools that he used to produce what I can only describe as some of the most beautifully neat and precise renditions of valve gear drawings and the like that I have ever seen.

He used a set of drawing instruments that had been passed on to him from his late father John Robinson. A set no doubt used at the turn of the century by that electrical engineer who did much of the work in converting over to electric power the many main line stations and buildings on the LNWR. The set is beautifully turned out in milled brass of changing section with copper plate etching and hand-profiled steel points. The maker was a company simply called 'Stanley'. In the set there are two large compasses, two small 'springbows', a couple of ivory-handled bow pens which he used for inking in the final drawings with Indian ink, a pair of wood and brass parallel rules and last but not least the most interesting (from my point of view) item. This is a pair of proportional dividers made by 'Elliott Brothers' of London to the same care of detail as the other parts of the set.

They are scaled for circles, solids and plans and perhaps the most intriguing thing about them is the marking 'Government of Japan'. They currently form part of my modeller's tool box as they have proved exceptionally useful in producing such articles as 4 mm finescale model signals from photographs. In most cases where one is trying to model an actual location the only thing you have as a guide is a photograph where certain components such as the arms, etc. are of a known length. Using a proportional divider one can quickly determine the near exact single plane sizes of the rest of the two dimensional subject. The whole set is still within its smart wooden box although the velvet lining is somewhat jaded and the key is missing. Most of the valve gear drawings were done with the purpose of staff training in mind as they were executed in a size suitable for display on a blackboard. Generally they were first drawn in pencil on cartridge paper of the old 'Half Imperial' size. Everything would then be inked in using the bow pens and the proprietary Indian inks available in art shops in the inter-war years. Where necessary, different colours were used to illustrate salient parts of the motion assemblies. Having looked through a number of his efforts now in my possession, it's fair to say that in many cases the drawings he used for the classes were 'blueprint' copies of Derby or Crewe

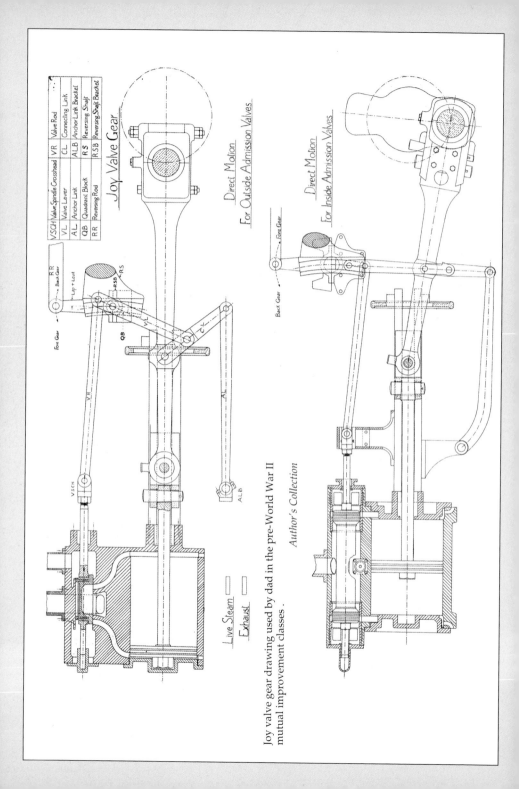

Joy Valve Gear

VSCH	Valve Spindle Crosshead	VR	Valve Rod
VL	Valve Lever	CL	Connecting Link
AL	Anchor Link	ALB	Anchor Link Bracket
QB	Quadrant Block	R S	Reversing Shaft
R R	Reversing Rod	RSB	Reversing Shaft Bracket

Direct Motion
For Outside Admission Valves

Direct Motion
For Inside Admission Valves

Live Steam
Exhaust

Joy valve gear drawing used by dad in the pre-World War II
mutual improvement classes .

Author's Collection

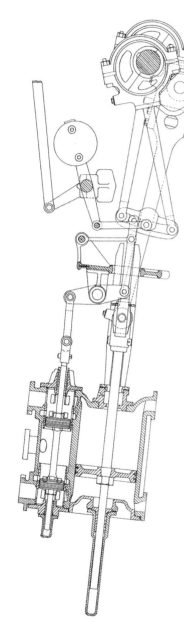

WITH ROCKING LEVER AND INSIDE ADMISSION PISTON VALVE

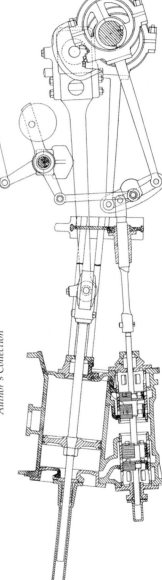

WITH OUTSIDE ADMISSION PISTON VALVE AND DOUBLE EXHAUST PORTS

Stephenson's Link valve gear. The lower assembly is similar to the arrangement used on the middle high pressure cylinder on the Johnson and Deeley Compounds.

Author's Collection

DAD HAD AN ENGINE SHED

originals. The exceptions to the rule inevitably occurred where there were no suitable copies of a valve gear type available, hence we see his superb renditions of Joy's valve gear in two formats and the Stephenson's Link motion, again in two formats, both drawn by the methods described and using the instruments mentioned.

Other drawings available include an improvement modification to an injector flap to prevent what had become a common and regular fault, that of sticking due to wear. Some of his contributions weren't always of a draughting nature, witness the letter to the chief operating manager, a Mr S.H. Fisher, LMSR, Watford 2. The letter is a suggestion, dated 22nd January, 1944, about basic improvements to prevent broken tender spring bolts from dropping into crucial areas of trackwork.

When the spring bolts of 4,000 gal standard tenders break they drop onto the permanent way with the possible danger of causing a derailment through becoming lodged in points or crossings. Also the material is lost and has to be replaced, i.e. the spring bolts, plate and container etc. So with a view to preventing these bolts from becoming displaced after fracturing I wish to suggest fixing a plate beneath ...

The somewhat tardy and patronizing reply (*reproduced below*) is probably unsurprising in itself. The story goes that the improvement was actually implemented some years later when the full seriousness of the recurrent problem was realised!

E.R.O. 51637

LONDON MIDLAND AND SCOTTISH RAILWAY COMPANY

S. H. FISHER,
Chief Operating Manager
Telephone—Watford 6464 Ext. ...46...
Telegrams—" Operating, Euston, London "

YOUR REFERENCE

CHIEF OPERATING MANAGER'S OFFICE,

L M S HEADQUARTERS.

WATFORD, Herts

OUR REFERENCE

COM/111/15036. ....7th May,............19 45.

PRIVATE AND CONFIDENTIAL.

Mr. J.E. Robinson,
   Fitter,
      Motive Power Depot,
         LLANDUDNO JUNCTION, LMS.14.

Dear Sir,

Referring to the suggestion you sent me some time ago in regard to the safety brackets under engine and tender spring bolts; consideration has been given to your suggestion, but if it were adopted it would weaken the "mutton chop" brackets, and in some cases there is not sufficient clearance within the loading gauge.

The failure of these bolts is not a frequent occurrence, and it is not, therefore, proposed to adopt your suggestion.

There is no doubt, however, that you have taken some trouble in preparing your drawings and I have, therefore, brought what you have said to the notice of the Management, and I am pleased to inform you it has been decided to grant you an interest award of 10/6d. I enclose a cheque for that amount herewith and shall be glad if you will acknowledge receipt to me by return and note that a suitable endorsement will be made on your service record card.

Yours faithfully,

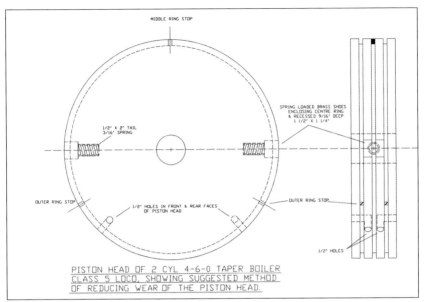

Plan illustrating dad's suggestion of 4th September, 1937 proposing a means to prevent wear on piston heads. *Author*

Another 'suggestion', dated 4th September, 1937 concerns a means to prevent wear of piston heads:

By drilling a ½″ hole on both sides of the piston head, near the bottom and just above the piston ring grooves to meet corresponding holes drilled vertically from the bottom between the inner and outer rings, thus allowing steam from each end alternately to lift the piston off the bottom of the cylinders. To prevent the steam escaping to the top half of the piston in the space between the rings, half way up on both sides insert brass pieces to fit closely between the rings and loaded with light springs to keep them against the cylinder walls. Stops should be fitted to keep the two outer rings near the bottom of the cylinders and that of the middle ring at the top.

On 30th October, 1942 the following suggestion was made concerning safety when opening smoke box doors on the Stanier taper boiler locomotives:

Sir,
I suggest that handles should be put on smoke box doors of tapered boiler engines as shown in the sketch.*
Recently there have been three accidents of the same nature one of which proved to be very serious. In two cases the men concerned were attempting to open the smoke box door by pulling on the dart lever attached to the centre of the door. When the door gave the lever spun round causing them to lose their balance and stumble over the main frame which projects across the foot frame at the front end. With a handle to grasp at the edge of the door where the leverage is required these accidents would not occur. The hand rail across the top of the door is out of reach when an effort is required to open the door'.

* NB: No sketch can be found but in my opinion the clarity of the description negates the need for one.

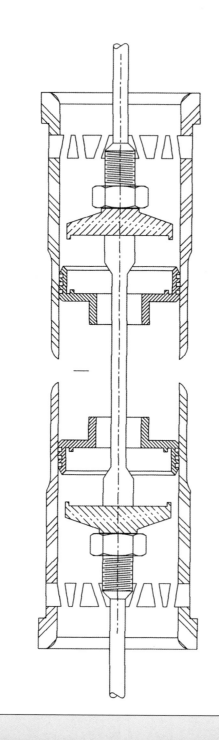

SECTIONAL VIEW OF TROFFINOF PISTON VALVE ASSEMBLY.

SHOWN IN LIVE STEAM SHUT OFF CONDITION.

Author

These suggestions, the results of which to the best of my knowledge (apart from the first) were not acted upon, I found amongst my father's ephemera in a little black note book, the ragged covers belie the interest and indeed value of the contents to anyone interested in keeping a preserved steam locomotive 'alive and well' today. It is a notebook partially filled in by his handwriting and pencil sketches of various items of a purely technical nature and he used it for reference purposes when lecturing to the mutual improvement classes at Llandudno Junction and later Mold Junction sheds. For interest I have included a number of short extracts concerning items not generally appreciated by those interested in the workings and maintenance of the steam locomotive.

The first concerns one of the probable but lesser known causes of boiler priming:

Over salty saturation/concentration of boiler water by the softening process giving a too alkaline and soapy effect coupled with suspended solid matter, causes viscosity of bubbles formed and so produces priming. To prevent over softened water forming sludge in the bottom of the boiler, use continuous blowdown.* Also an exhaust steam working injector carries oil in suspension from the cylinders, therefore requiring thorough separation, as since the adoption of atomizers, the cylinder lubrication oil is broken up more finely and a quantity is passed over to the exhaust injector as an emulsion in the steam. This emulsion is very difficult to break down and requires an additional grease separator. Priming is probably the cause of excessive wear of piston rings owing to the soapy nature of the foam carried into the cylinders, soapy and alkaline water being more destructive to the oil lubrication on the cylinder walls than clean water. That the piston wear on engines fitted with exhaust steam injectors is far greater than those with only live steam injectors, seems to point to oil as the second factor necessary to promote priming!

The second interesting note concerns the advantages of Troffinof valves:

Piston valves with loose heads which remain in the middle of the steam chest during coasting form a by-pass between the cylinder ends thus saving the cylinders from being cooled off by air from the snifters and flue gases drawn down the exhaust pipe.

The third note concerned lap and lead and at this point it might prove beneficial if we examine some of his notes that concern the meaning of those oft used terms 'lap and lead':

Lap is the amount by which the slide valve overlaps each steam port when the valve is in its mid position and is the means provided for working the steam expansively by cutting it off before the end of the stroke, as after the steam has been cut off the valve has to travel an amount equal to the lap before it opens the port on the inner edge to the exhaust. The piston during the same time has traversed over the period of expansion.

Lead is to ensure that the boiler pressure is built up in the clearance volume by the commencement of the stroke thus preventing drawing caused by the gradual opening of the valve, also it helps to cushion the piston. From the sketch it is clear that the valve fulfills the following necessary conditions:-

---

* I assume this term refers to regular operation of the blow down valve thus releasing the boiler pressure when the engine is 'shedded' prior to a boiler washing out operation, thus blowing out the sludges that build up on a very regular basis.

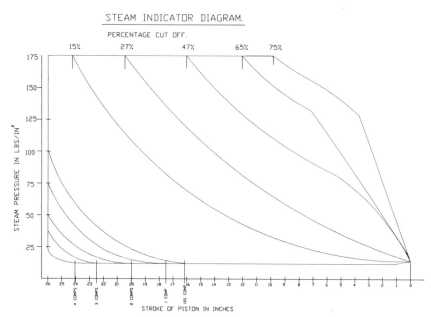

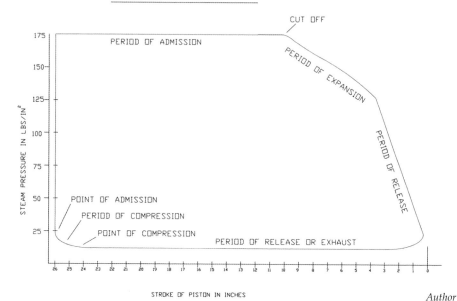

Author

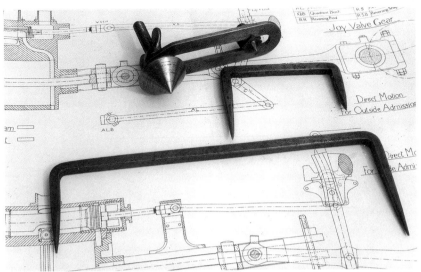

The three part tool that my father made whilst he was at Llandudno Junction shed. He once described it as 'A tool for setting the valves on the inside cylinder of a Scot relative to the settings of the valves on the two outside cylinders'. Well if anyone's got a 'Scot' that needs its valves setting they are welcome to try it out! As can be seen it is essentially a short adjustable trammel with a large coned bolt at one end, the cone's offset from the trammel can be locked with a wing nut. On one side is stamped 'No. 3' whilst the other side carries his initials 'J.R.'. *Author*

(1) It will not admit steam into both ends of the cylinder at the same time.
(2) It allows exhaust steam to escape from one end before admitting live steam to the other end and so reduces the back pressure.
(3) It does not allow live steam to enter the exhaust from the cylinders without it first doing work.
(4) By notching the engine up the valve travel is reduced causing the post opening to be diminished giving an earlier cut off allowing for expansive working.

My dad's suggestion was:

Long stroke piston valves as used in all modern engines with about 1½" lap + ⅛" exhaust clearance and 6½" travel in full gear are designed to give the best possible indicator diagram when well notched up. i.e. although using the steam as economically as possible by expansion, there are no sudden changes of pressure which set up undue stresses in the motion and bearings. The advantages of increased lap in steam distribution are to increase the valve opening at every range of cut-off and to increase the velocity of the valve at the periods of opening and closing and finally to increase the exhaust port opening so that a full port is available when notched up. When drifting/coasting notch up to 45% cut-off to prevent drawing gases down the blast pipe.

It will be noticed from the diagram that by notching up, all the different operations are advanced owing to the shorter travel of the valve.

Exhaust lap would also prolong the period of expansion by delaying the exhaust, but it would cause compression to start earlier at the end of the stroke and is seldom used in locomotives, owing to the excessive compression produced. Exhaust Clearance is in some cases necessary to prevent excessive compression when notched up, but it has a tendency to cause back pressure and so a 'hump' in the exhaust curve when working slowly and in full gear.

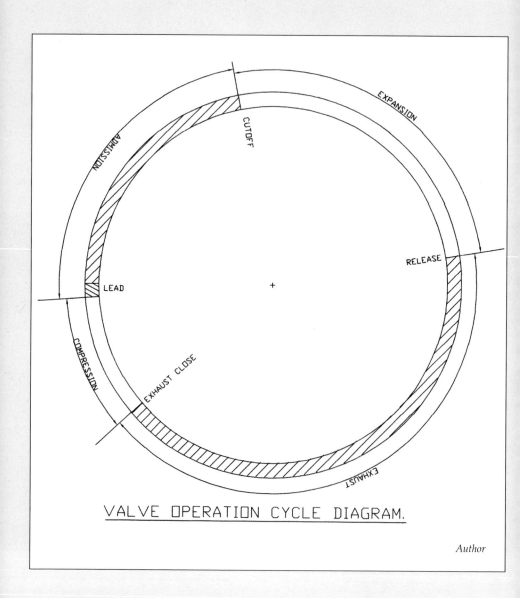

VALVE OPERATION CYCLE DIAGRAM.

Author

Chapter Seven

Mold Junction, 1952-1960

An important development, that had taken place earlier on that I have not made any reference to, mainly because it concerned family and not railway matters, was the injury sustained by my mother whilst putting up 'Blackout' curtains at the outbreak of war. She slipped and fell injuring her leg severely on the rough and germ-ridden edge of the kitchen sink. Remember the sinks in those days were not the smooth stainless steel units we have now. Apart from some initial first aid administered at the time of the accident nothing further was done. Alas, that was to prove grossly inadequate as within a period of months infection set in and so began a hellishly painful and traumatic period of hospitalization, firstly in the local hospital at Llandudno and later (after the war) at Fazakerley, Liverpool. After several operations she was rendered to a wheelchair and during her clinical trials and tribulations she went to stay with one of her aunts for a period of recuperation. Now this lady was a widow who lived with her two sons in the village of Broughton which lies about four miles west of Chester just off the A55 road to Conway and the North Wales coast.

It seemed at the time to my father that she was never going to get better, but after a short sabbatical in what was then a small village on the Welsh border the change in her was little short of remarkable! So after a year or so she was returned for another hopefully beneficial spell of a couple of weeks. Again she returned much better for the embracing air off the Cheshire Plains. Dad in his infinite wisdom put it down to the change in air and water, saying that the sea air of the Junction was too relaxing for her and the water too soft!

Rightly or not, he was convinced and whilst at that 'Glory Hole' of Sowerby Bridge decided that if he got the chance of a move back to his old area, preferably the Chester end, he would jump at it. An offer of the position of shed master at Goole on the banks of the Humber came along but he stuck out for what was to be the ultimate move of his career.

Early in 1952 he heard on the 'grapevine' that Ernest Crofts of Mold Junction shed was about to retire. Without further ado he put forward his application to be his replacement and was successful. He commenced there as shed master in May of that year with his precursor staying on for about six weeks to show him the ropes. He moved his digs from Mrs Taylor at Sowerby Bridge to Mr & Mrs Bradshaw's of Saltney Ferry Terrace, which was just over the bridge from the shed. Mr Crofts, incidentally, was to become a close family friend for the rest of his natural.

The importance of Mold Junction (6B) shed was essentially in its freight engine stud and what was for the area one of the finest locomotive handling facilities available. Whilst the nearby Chester (6A) shed mainly served the passenger requirements of the area and had a larger covered eight-road area, Mold Junction also of eight covered roads was blessed with that monument of progress, the semi-automatic coaling plant (of LMS design). This of course enabled a rapid turn around of locomotive servicing and was to prove in the

Goole shed in 1950. This is the ex-L&Y outpost on Humberside where my father almost wound up. How different our family life would have been if that had been the case!

R.S. Carpenter Photos

Mold Junction on 22nd September, 1952. The photograph was taken shortly after the commencement of my father's tenure. *From left to right are*: Fred Roberts, clerk; Fred Butler; Ernie Crofts, the recently retired shed master; Tom Jones, running shed foreman; Alan Roberts, chief clerk; J.E. Robinson, shed master.   *Author's Collection*

shed's final and busiest decade of its existence invaluable to say the least. As with all sheds with a pre-war concrete coaling plant the structure, which had a height something in excess of 80 ft, was a local landmark. Much has been said in articles more superior and technically detailed than this about the shed, its purpose and position in the general scheme of things so I will confine my narrative to those matters which concern my own limited experiences, memories and knowledge.

For the first two years my father lodged at the Bradshaws. Mr Bradshaw was himself a retired driver and so had lots of tales with which to amuse his new guest. At this time an earnest search began to find suitable housing for the family, which was still resident at Llandudno Junction. The 'railway houses' in the adjacent Ewart Street and North Street were the obvious first place to look, these were typical old terraced LNWR houses which were less than inviting with the customary outside loo, etc. Also the location 'didn't qualify on health grounds' as being at sea level and very near to the River Dee at Saltney Ferry; notwithstanding this my mother would not entertain living in a house with outside 'facilities' anyway.

Hawarden Rural District Council were engaged in building a fine estate of houses in the favoured location of Broughton village. These were primarily constructed to house the swelling ranks of workers and their families at the nearby De Havilland Aircraft Company's works. One of the footplate inspectors based at the shed was a member of the said council's housing committee and a few words in the right ears quickly secured the 'Swiss Family' a four-bedroomed terraced house in Fairfield Road, with a nice open aspect at the rear. Indeed, yours truly quickly found that if he stood on the upstairs toilet seat a distant view of the 6B coaling plant could be gained! So in April 1954 with the aid of Pickfords and my uncle's Standard 'Flying Nine' we moved in lock, stock, and tea chests and with a little help from a boiler washer on his afternoon off we were safely ensconced in our new abode by nightfall.

Whilst Broughton wasn't exactly next door to the shed (thank goodness), with the aid of a pre-war Raleigh push bike, replete with Sturmey Archer three-speed gears (crossbar mounted selector), dad was able to get to work each day by cycling the mile or so to Broughton & Bretton station where the venerable machine would be stowed in the ground floor of the signal box. Then he boarded the 8.20 am to the next station up the line, Saltney Ferry, which was adjacent to the shed. This train was frequently hauled by one of Mold Junction's own Fowler '4F' locomotives.

My first visit to the shed came later that same summer when my mother and I (remember I was just five years old) took a bus to Lane End, Saltney Ferry. From here it was a short walk of about 400 yards to the shed (road) entrance at the foot of the road overbridge that carried the B5129 over the Chester to Holyhead main line and on to Sandycroft and Queensferry. The visit as I recall was an invitation to tea from Mrs Bradshaw, my dad's former landlady. So our first port of call was my dad's office which lay at the rear of the shed down a narrow corridor which led into a built-up archway of the road overbridge. At the end of the corridor a door opened into the chief clerk's office whilst the door on the left opened into that most hallowed of places, the shedmaster's office.

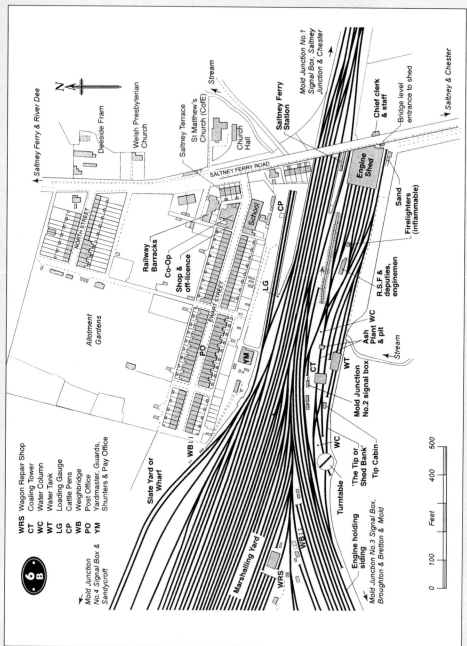

R. Carvell

Mold Junction shed track plan, *circa* 1961.

As mentioned in the text this LMS-built coaling plant was the only one of its type installed on the Chester-Holyhead line. Here a wagon can be seen secured on the lifting hoist and on its way up to the tipping hood where it will be canted over onto its side to deposit its contents into a massive concrete hopper. Note the electric capstan in the foreground used for hauling the wagons onto the lifting platform. Ex-GWR 'Grange' class 4-6-0 No. 6821 *Leaton Grange* is positioned with its tender in the receiving position beneath the 'jiggler'.

- E.N. Kneale

The first of two views taken around Spike Island. Saltney Terrace, was where my father lodged with the Bradshaws. *Author*

Ewart Street, replete with its school and shop. We could have lived here. *Author*

That office, which I was later to visit many times during the next 12 years, stuck me as a dark but curiously comfortable place with its single bay window and superb uninterrupted view of the trains passing by on the Chester-Holyhead main line outside. It had a high mantle piece on which was perched the omnipresent pipe rack displaying the usual complement of essential 'tools for deep cogitation'. The desk was somewhat elaborate for an LNWR outpost, but judging by its age and obvious signs of wear and tear, had found its way there as a 'hand me down' via the stores van from some other more important enclave eons previously.

As one walked back down the corridor into the main shed, the stores lay on the right of the passageway, this like most of its genre had a small hatch window (the likes of which a young apprentice would be sent to wait at all day for a 'long stand'!). Opposite and to the right of the stores window was enshrined the sand drier, or 'Rocket' as the men termed it. I say enshrined because it always, to my mind at least, seemed to permanently reside in the middle of a veritable mountain of sand. The drivers' mess room was next to this device and formed one of the 'under arches' of the road over bridge. The fitter's cabin was a timber affair resembling a very grubby looking greenhouse and adjacent to this and against the south wall of the shed was the driver's locker room or 'lobby'. The shed had eight roads which lay under a modernized but truncated roof, so short in fact the longest road would only house a buffered up class '5' and 'Humpy'* under cover. The outside of the building still retained pits in each road, an area known as the 'Shed Bank' which would have originally been under the old north light roof. In common with most non-through road sheds the interior had a continuously smoky atmosphere (especially on a Sunday morning when most of my subsequent visits were made).

The thing that sticks most prominently in my mind about that first ever visit to an engine shed was the sheer size of the locomotives within. To a child who had previously only viewed a locomotive close up from a station platform they seemed absolutely enormous and the climb up into the cab was a most perilous undertaking! This memory is often stirred today when I hear comments from people who may have visited a preserved railway or 'shed' and encountered a steam locomotive at close quarters for perhaps the first time in their unenlightened lives.

That first visit was cut short by the arrival of Mr Bradshaw who insisted on taking me down to the 'real' Saltney Ferry for a trip across the River Dee on the then still-existing ferry boat service. As a concrete footbridge has extended across the river for more than 20 years now, not many people will remember that for intrepid travellers it was once the practice to hail the ferryman from the 'Welsh' side of the river by signalling one's desire to cross by waving clearly from the landing stage. He would then come out of his hut on the opposite side of the river and pilot his 'Seagull'-powered outboard-motored rowing boat out across to meet you. That first crossing was to me an adventure in itself because we were accompanied by at least two cyclists who with their machines perched precariously upright across the crossbeams of the boat hung on to them as we bucked and rolled in a stiff breeze across the part of the River Dee. This is as straight as a die due to canalizing in the 18th century from Connah's Quay to

* Humpy was the Mold Junction (6B) name for a 'Jinty' or Fowler 0-6-0 '3F' tank engine.

Saltney Ferry, today there is no longer a ferry.

Author

Saltney. That most pleasant of afternoons was finished with afternoon tea at the Bradshaws before retiring to the single island platform of Saltney Ferry station where my dad joined us for the short journey home on the 5.22 pm train to Broughton & Bretton.

Although in the early days visits to the shed were few and far between, they tended to increase in frequency as I became more interested in matters of railways and steam locomotives. To railway servants of my father's seniority the job and the company invariably took first place in their lives with their homes and families coming a sometimes grudging second. This was exemplified by the seven day presence that he always put in at the shed. It didn't matter how smoothly things were running it was imperative to put an hour or so in on a Sunday morning, unpaid of course! This was the time that yours truly usually chose to tag along for the ride, as there was never a Sunday train service on the Mold and Denbigh branch in its later years of existence. The sort of activities one might see at the shed on a Sunday morning usually centred around the regular chores of boiler washing and work entailing motion stripping for running repairs that could obviously be done over a weekend. Perhaps the most memorable of activities was that of coal heaving on the long coal storage stacks that ran along the back road of the shed yard. It should be appreciated that on Sundays the shed was 'locked in' as No. 2 box was inoperative and the only locomotive in steam would be a 'Humpy' which would be employed by the shed turner to rearrange engines rostered to be first, second, third, etc., off the shed on the first shift on that Sunday night and Monday morning. I distinctly remember spending many a Sunday morning watching a 'Humpy' hauling three or four dead engines in and out of the various shed roads, with the cylinder taps all set open wheezing and hissing on each locomotive as they eased slowly past.

I think it was in 1959 that 6B got its first diesel shunter, an 0-6-0 mechanical drive Drewry in an all-green livery, no yellow stripes or panels in those days. Well this was the new toy and I personally got several rides in the cab up and down the back road between the shed and the turntable. However, I don't ever remember the thing having the guts to haul dead engines up and down like the 'Humpys' did! I think it spent most of its time pottering about in the slate yard before being replaced by the larger 350 bhp 0-6-0 diesel-electric shunters, now called class '08'.

Mold Junction Allocation 1959

Class '3F' 0-6-0T	47615, 47646, 47650
Class '4F' 0-6-0	43908, 44065, 44073, 44117, 44493
Class '5P/4F' 2-6-0	42945, 42965, 42971, 42976, 42982, 42960, 42967, 42973, 42981
Class '5' 4-6-0	44800, 44971, 45001, 45028, 45043, 45055, 45130, 45247, 45275, 45325, 45345
Class '8F' 2-8-0	48246, 48259, 48458
Class 'WD' 2-8-0 'Austerity'	90147, 90157, 90178, 90187, 90227, 90242, 90257, 90317, 90423, 90532, 90566, 90606,90702

Total 44 locomotives

Source: Steam Archive Services

The following year (1960) the allocation list was swollen to number some 60 engines which included, unusually for a predominantly freight shed, four 'Patriot' ('Baby Scots') from Carnforth. They arrived on 23rd January, 1960 and three departed to Warrington (Dallam) exactly three months later, and one went to Rugby on the same day, 23rd April, 1960. They were as follows: Nos. 45501 *St. Dunstan's*, 45511 *Isle of Man*, 45546 *Fleetwood*, 45548 *Lytham St. Annes* (to Rugby). No. 45501 was one of the two original engines rebuilt from ex-LNWR 'Claughton' class locomotives.

For one memorably sunny afternoon in the summer of 1959 my father invited my pal and I down to the shed (we were given notes to take to school for exclusion from afternoon lessons) in order to view the contents of the enginemen's instruction van that had arrived from Derby a couple of days previously. At this point it must be said that because from an early age I had expressed more than a passing interest in things mechanical, especially steam engines, dad had taken it upon himself to educate me on the workings of the steam locomotive, he even built a working model of Walchaerts valve gear out of my Meccano to assist in my enlightenment. His friend Max Dunn frowned upon this and believed that interest beyond that of modelling and drawing should not be encouraged 'lest the lad should choose a railway career'! Anyway, right or wrong, the offer of this visit filled me with thrilled anticipation. My friend, David Willoughby who lived on a smallholding in nearby Bretton and who also had a passion for 'things mechanical' persuaded his parents to give him the afternoon off school. And so on that balmy afternoon we set off after the lunch break from Broughton County Primary School to cycle the two miles to the shed. On arrival we found the place

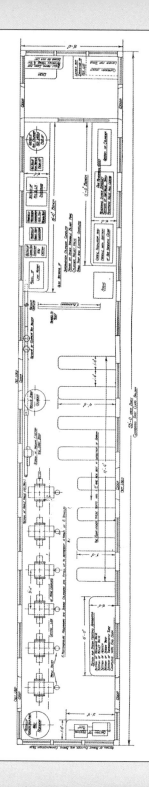

Layout plan of LMS instruction coach taken from *Locomotive Running Shed Management* (Paterson & Webster).

positively buzzing with activity and I particularly remember a number of ex-LNWR 'Super D' 0-8-0s being on shed. I also recall my father breaking up a 'Mothers Meeting' that was taking place on one of the said locomotive's footplates! Just why those guys chose such a cramped footplate to have their tea and gossip on I shall never know.

We eventually boarded the instruction van which was parked in the No. 8 road (nearest the station). From the outside it looked thoroughly underwhelming, an old period I LMS coach, covered in years of filth and grime no doubt aquired by standing outside engine sheds. But on ascending the small step ladder at the end of the coach, one entered a veritable Aladdin's Cave. There was all sorts of equipment, most of which at the time I had no recognition of whatsoever. There was what appeared to be a small classroom with benches and a blackboard, alongside which was what I now know to be a full Westinghouse brake system. But the items that really caught my attention where the board and plinth-mounted models of different types of locomotive valve gears. These were obviously designed to demonstrate the methods of valve setting and the workings of reversing gear etc., and could be made to operate by turning a handle at the wheel or eccentric/crank end of the apparatus. All parts were beautifully polished in bright chromium-plated steel and were an absolute delight to 'play with'! After about an hour of intense and unchaperoned amusement David and I were offered a cup of tea by the gentleman in charge of the ensemble. He had a small cabin at the end of the coach which housed a sink, a small kettle and all the necessary accoutrements that made the place a travelling home. Most people have heard the term 'railway tea', I can honestly say that never before or since have I tasted a brew so foul and strong that one could literally stand the proverbial spoon up in it! As I recall we both quietly tipped our cupfuls out of the open window when he wasn't looking. Anyway my dad came to our rescue shortly after that and for being 'good boys' we were put 'out of the way' on a Stanier '8F' footplate for the next hour.

The '8F' was in low steam and the interesting thing about it was that it was a star-marked engine fitted with a Fowler tender. The star above the cabside numerals indicated that it was balanced by the works for the higher speeds of fitted freight and parcels working.

I must confess that to me one of the more attractive aspects of the Mold Junction scenario was its position regarding the Mold and Denbigh branch. The line in its later years at least, never produced much of a contribution in the way of passenger receipts and the passenger trains themselves reflected this as they were rarely made up of more than two or three suburban coaches. Most of the motive power was provided by Chester depot in the form of 2-6-4T and 2-6-2T engines of the usual Fowler, Stanier, Fairburn, British Railways (BR) or Ivatt types. However, there were one or two passenger turns that fell to the lot of 6B.

My school in those days was blessed with an uninterrupted easterly view across the fields of Broughton to the line as it emerged from bridge No. 1, the brick-built single-span bridge that carried the lane connecting Broughton to Bretton (nicknamed 'Timbuctoo Bridge' by my father), to climb the short 1 in 100 bank that led to a descent to the bottom of the infamous Kinnerton bank. Every

'Timbuctoo Bridge', Broughton in 1996. Despite the devestation of the area by the construction of the A55 road and its attendant junction with Broughton village, the old bridge still remains in place, now just carrying a footpath to the new retail park. No. 1 overbridge on the Chester, Mold & Denbigh line: the Glynn Arms which was adjacent to Broughton & Bretton station can just be seen beneath the arch.   *Author*

Kinnerton bank in 1996 and the skewed twin arches of the first of the 'three bridges' situated about halfway up the 1 in 43 bank. The distant signal for Dodds siding was just to the left of where the photographer was standing. Today one can walk up the bank from near the village on a footpath, but beyond the bridge the cutting has been filled in, making it difficult to follow the course of the formation.   *Author*

weekday including Saturdays the 3.32 pm from Chester would come thundering under that bridge at just after 3.45 pm. I use the word thundering advisedly as it was always hauled by a Mold Junction Fowler '4F'. That was precisely the time that we came out of school and one day we heard two council workmen exclaim, 'There goes the quart four, it's time to go!' From that time on we called the train the 'Quart Four'. If I read the shed diagrams correctly that engine was on turn 10 which basically allotted two of the class to the branch workings six days a week. Another regular 6B passenger working, which on fine summer afternoons my mates and I would view from 'Timbuctoo Bridge', was the 3.35 pm from Denbigh which was often worked by a 6B Stanier Mogul on turn 112.

It has to be said that despite the relative unimportance of the line you could set your watch by the punctuality of its traffic. Naturally the main interest was the freight traffic and of course it must be remembered that what went down the line did not necessarily come back up as there were busy interchange sidings at Hope with the 'North Eastern'* plus the possibility of traffic going on to the Rhyl-Corwen branch. On taking the 'throne' at Mold Junction in 1952 my dad inherited a footplate pass to Brymbo via Mold and Coed Talon: his joke always was, 'Look at this! You've got to walk the last four miles, good eh?' The Coed Talon to Brymbo section had been lifted literally within a few days of him receiving the pass! Notwithstanding the joke he certainly got a fair bit of use out of it (not that he needed to show it) as the trackwork up in those hillside sidings was in a parlous state and breakdowns were common.

Breakdowns

This brings us to the above subject which, in the book on shed management, has been   described as, 'Work which is invariably interesting, and often unconventional'. Try telling that to a cold and hungry breakdown crew working in foul conditions in the early hours of a winter's morning! To be fair, in my father's case volunteering to be a member of the breakdown crew in the early part of his career did have a certain amount of the 'Gung Ho' about it, although as mentioned earlier in the text, no doubt the opportunity to boost one's pay was the chief incentive. However, the duty that fell to the shedmaster's lot was in most individual cases the greatest bane of their undertaking!

Mold Junction in common with most main line motive power depots had not just a breakdown gang of about six men plus the 'Gaffer' but they also had at their disposal a fully-equipped breakdown van. This was normally kept, when not in use, at the bottom of the end (No. 1) road of the shed. It was essentially a tool van with mess facilities for the crew. The tools mainly comprised of a collection of jacks, packing (a motley collection of old shortened sleepers and steel plates and blocks), and various types of slewing gear. The van was an old 59 ft LMS corridor full brake with a double width reinforced sliding door inserted in each side. Whether the vehicle ever had a livery is not known, but to me it just looked dirty black and very uninviting! This van would be towed to the site of the breakdown by whatever locomotive was in steam and 'available'. Serious jobs, such as a major collision or a locomotive on its side for instance,

* The ex-Wrexham, Mold & Connah's Quay (Great Central, later London & North Eastern Railway (LNER)) line between Dee Marsh & Wrexham.

would be thankfully delegated to the Chester crew who had a 35 ton Cowans Sheldon steam crane at their disposal. However, the decision to call out the 'Heavy Mob' was often taken only after the 6B team had arrived on the scene and decided the job was beyond their capabilities!

In all the years of my father's career, 47 in total, he never once complained out loud about being called out on a breakdown, although I feel that, especially in the final years, he must have inwardly cursed beyond measure the incompetence of the individuals who put locomotive and wagons 'on the floor' in the middle of the night. Generally if a wagon was derailed at night in a position not likely to cause an obstruction the matter of re-railing was left until the morning. I remember with profound sympathy, the times when after a particularly gruelling day the phone would ring and he would have to don his railway coat and leggings (in inclement conditions) and make his way back to the shed possibly not to return until the early hours of the next day. One particularly bad night during that hellish winter of 1962-63 he arrived home from work at about 9.00 pm having attended a breakdown in deep snow at Hendre Sidings (just beyond Rhydymwyn on the Denbigh line). He came in blue with cold and having eaten a late dinner had a hot bath and retired to bed.

Sometime later I recall awaking to a vibrating noise, I lay there in my warm bed gradually coming to my senses when I sat up with a jerk! It was the phone ringing, pulling on my dressing gown I went down to answer it, knowing before I picked it up what it would be. A tired voice on the other end said, 'Tell Mr Robinson there's an engine on the floor at the West End, I've called the rest of the gang out, thank you', click and the line went dead. I didn't even get a

The Chester breakdown crane in the mid-1960s.   *Cleve Jones*

chance to ask any questions, let alone call my dad to the phone. I think the caller (no doubt the duty running shift foreman) was just thankful that I had answered the phone! So it was up to yours truly to rouse him; I have to confess that I seriously toyed with the idea of just going back to bed but I knew that the phone would ring again in another hour or so and then there would be hell to pay. So up to my parents room I went to find my dad fast asleep, my mother was deaf so there was no chance of her hearing the phone anyway. I shook him and he awoke, 'Sorry dad but it's a breakdown again, an engine on the floor at the West End'. Without even a scowl he just told me to get back to bed and proceeded to get dressed, it was 3.15 am and I was glad to climb back into my bed. Remember, by then he was over 60 years of age!

A week or so after that more fresh snow had fallen and he attended another breakdown at Hendre Sidings. This time the sun was shining and the snow was so deep that when they got to Mold they reversed the engine (a class '5') around to the back of the breakdown coach. My dad was scared of derailing the engine in the snow drifts, there was no snow plough available, and so the coach was put in the lead. If that derailed they could all go home on the engine! Beyond Alyn Tinplate box the whole area was just a vast sea of snow with no sign of a railway in existence (a bit like today!). My dad just hung out of the leading door of the van waving the engine slowly forward. He said of the experience at the time that it was like being in charge of an Icebreaker in the Antarctic. Well they got to their breakdown, I'm afraid time has erased the details, and they got home in time for tea. Obviously feeling braver they had bulldozed their way back to Mold engine leading. It went on like that all through that winter, if it wasn't frozen points it was something else but it was never the fault of the signalman, shunter, driver or fireman *et al*!

In the summer of 1964 I actually attended a breakdown that occurred one evening at the shed itself. Again the phone had rung but not until we had finished our evening meal, the weather was warm and sunny so I asked if I could come down to the shed to witness the proceedings as such opportunities were for me rare indeed (why didn't I take a camera?). On arrival we were directed by one of the men down to the turntable where we found two class '5s' in a somewhat sorry state. One was coming engine first off the table and heading for the coaling plant when it was struck on its front left side by another also bound for the coaling plant on the turntable by-pass road.

In the split second it took for the drivers to apply the brakes the engines had forced each other over into a precarious angle and had gouged off both opposing cylinder wrappers and considerable damage had been done to both front buffer beams and running plates. As far as I can recall the valve gears had miraculously escaped damage.

I stayed for a couple of hours watching dad and the 'gang' setting up the required packing and slewing gear. One thing that sticks firmly in my mind was the cool professionalism with which they handled what could have been a very dangerous situation should either engine have slipped off its packing, as this could have pushed the other into a potentially toppling position. I left the scene as the light faded but dad was home with all done and dusted by 11.00 pm. The two engines had to go into the works to have the damage attended to.

On the evening of 16th July, 1954 my father arrived home at his usual time and reported that earlier that day one of the 'jets' from De Havilland's had collided with the top of an engine's tender and that the aircraft had come off by far the worst in the altercation! My latter day investigations turned up this photograph which shows that indeed he was right! The aircraft, a 'Sea Venom Mk 20' (Reg. WM544, Works No. 12627, believed to be for the Royal Navy) is shown after the crash being de-fuelled in the presence of the company fire officers. A complete 'write off', it was on its final approach to runway 23 when its undercarriage struck the top of the tender of a Stanier '8F' locomotive that was standing with its train on the up slow awaiting the road to cross over into the West End yard. The locomotive crew were driver William Williams and fireman William Roberts of Llandudno Junction shed, the engine number and home shed as yet have evaded detection. The 'Sea Venom' crew were test pilot Jimmy Phillips, who went on to further his career with Airbus Industrie at Toulouse and observer Tony Chalk who sadly later perished in another accident with chief test pilot Alan Brandon in March 1966 when their 'Vampire's' 'Goblin' engine suffered a 'flame out' over the Berwyn mountains. As an apprentice I was chosen to be a member of the search party, but local people found the bodies before we had time to get under way. On both occasions it was known that the flight crews did not wear parachutes, indeed Alan Brandon was so tall that he would not consider ejection from the Vampire & Venom jets due to the danger of losing his legs under the dashboards which were very close to the front edge of the ejector seats.

Courtesy of De Havilland Aircraft Museum Trust

Breakdowns were mostly mundane and indeed too numerous to mention, but there were the very unusual occurrences which stand out. Like the time in July 1954 when the pilot of one of the small jet fighters (a 'Sea Venom') from the nearby De Havilland factory got it wrong coming into land across the main line and took the bottom out of his fuselage on the top of an engine's tender. Needless to say the jet came off worst, the pilot survived the collision, but whether he survived the wrath of the chief test pilot is not on record! The footplate crew was from Llandudno Junction and they were badly shocked but unharmed.

An event which provided some amusement was the re-railing of some runaway vans at the brickworks sidings just across the main road from Coed Talon. The trackbed of the line to Brymbo carried on straight ahead but the remaining line ran to the right into the yard of a works that specialized in the production of fine stone dust as used in domestic talcum powder. The trucks had become engulfed in the said product and by the time the 'gang' had finished both they and the 'Gaffer' had become engulfed in it too! Needless to say they got a right ribbing when they returned to the shed looking like snowmen. One can only surmise that it was fortuitous that the powder was unscented otherwise they would have got a shade more than a ribbing when they got home!

My dad was never a particularly demonstrative father and, to my mind at least, he spent far more time chastising my misdemeanours than he ever did praising my achievements - probably because they were few and far between anyway. However, there was at least one occasion when he took advantage of an entirely unusual opportunity on my behalf. It was probably the autumn of 1957 or 1958 when in the early hours he was cycling home from yet another night time breakdown and there was a strong wind of gale force blowing. From Mold Junction he would have cycled up the 'Back Lane' into our estate, this chestnut tree-lined avenue was about half a mile long and beside it was sited my primary school. The road was littered with wind-felled conkers, horse chestnuts to give them the proper name, and so having arrived home at about 4 am and despite his tiredness he collected an old shoe box and returned to the lane to fill it up! You can imagine my reaction when I awoke that morning to find the overflowing box on the kitchen table. Not too many conkers left for the other kids either!

The greatest source of breakdowns at Mold Junction was without doubt the large marshalling yard adjacent to the shed yard. It was here that all freight traffic destined to or from any place on the Chester-Holyhead line was made up into trains for the individual destinations along the line. Freight for Bangor, Anglesey or the Afonwen line would be sent as a complete train from Mold Junction for individual sorting at Menai Bridge yard. Whereas traffic for Llandudno/Colwyn Bay/Blaenau Ffestiniog, etc. would be sent to Llandudno Junction for sorting. Freight for the then numerous private sidings that existed between Mold Junction and Rhyl would be marshalled into trains for the daily 'Pick-up' goods that ran twixt the two places. Apart from the station goods yards along the line there was considerable traffic emerging from Dundas sidings between Sandycroft & Queensferry, Muspratts at Flint, ICI at Greenfield (Holywell Junction), Mostyn Ironworks, Point of Ayr Colliery etc., etc. The maximum permitted load from Abergele to Mold Junction yard was 90 wagons.

Airfield straight in 1996. The down slow line had been lifted and the up slow was out of use despite the continued gleam from the Mold Junction up distant light. This was the location where my father carried out the dreaded sight testing of drivers and firemen. The point where the line curves to the left is just beyond where No. 4 signal box and its attendant home gantry was. *Author*

Mold Junction slate yard in 1996, by this time just a parking place for permanent way department wagons. All traces of the East End yard have been replaced by bushes and trees. This view is looking in the down direction, the white and red aircraft hangars originally the property of RAF Hawarden, then De Havilland's and Hawker Siddelely, now belong to Raytheon Corporate Jets. *Author*

For operational reasons the yard was split into four sectors, three of which had a shunting engine and crew (which included one or sometimes two shunters) allocated to it. If one was to travel down the main line (North Wales-bound) the largest sector of the yard was on the left: this comprised firstly the East End which led to the West End which subsequently led back out onto the main line again at No. 3 box. These two sectors were by far the largest and comprised 11 loop roads, which were worked back to back by shunters at both the East and West ends. At the far side of the loop roads lay five sidings which led out to the West End, trains being made up for their directional destinations respectively. Naturally great care had to be exercised by the opposing teams of shunters to avoid end-on collisions! On the up side of the main line lay the slate yard that by the post-war years had become an anachronism. This purpose-built yard had seven siding roads running between wharfs leading out in the up direction into a very long headshunt running alongside the main line to eventually reach some factories in nearby Saltney. Like the previously mentioned Deganwy Quay it would have handled the output from the Penrhyn quarries at Bethesda plus some of the Dinorwic materials that didn't go by sea to their intended destinations. Most of the Blaenau Ffestiniog traffic was siphoned away via the competing Great Western and Festiniog railways through Bala and Portmadoc respectively. However, the optimistic LNWR built a fine transhipment and sorting yard complete with wharfs and loading bays. Slate traffic was stored and sorted and it clearly was an extra service that the railway company provided at this point for the slate quarry companies. However, post-war it was used to sort out the local freight bound for Saltney and Chester, etc. Again this yard was always busy and had a shunting engine and crew allocated to it.

The fourth sector of the yard was referred to as the Mold End, this as the name suggests led in the direction of the Mold branch and lay alongside it. It comprised of two loop roads leading out of the East End plus two siding roads which all ran out onto the Mold line at Mold Junction No. 3 box. It was here that the freight for the Mold and Denbigh line was made up. The East End shunter was invariably detailed to handle this work as required. The West and Mold ends were linked by a two-road loop curve of 10 chains radius called the 'Circle' that effectively formed a triangle. Down trains entering the yards from the east would run into the Mold branch and then set back into the Mold End from where the engine would either go 'on shed' for turning etc., or proceed to the next job as the case may be.

Freight trains taking the Mold & Denbigh line would naturally depart from the Mold End and the East End shunter would make up these trains from stock previously deposited there or the other parts of the yard depending on its origin. One of the more interesting workings up the Mold branch was the thrice-weekly morning '10.40 Mold'. This was a 2-8-0 '8F' or 'Austerity'-worked 'Turn 101' on the shed diagrams and was banked by another similar locomotive up to Pen-y-Ffordd, whereupon the train engine would give one crow of his whistle signalling the banker was no longer required; the latter in turn would reply with two crows. The train engine then replied with two crows and the banker again replied this time with one crow before slowing to a stop outside the signal

Fireman Cleve Jones stands next to '8F' class 2-8-0 No. 48648 of Llandudno Junction shed at United Colliery, Gresford. *Bill Roberts*

Ex-LMS 'Jubilee' class 4-6-0 No. 45572 *Eire*, all the way from St Phillip's Marsh shed in Bristol, forms the backdrop at Mold Junction shed. *From left to right are*: driver Bill Roberts (of Holyhead), fitters Les Macey and Jack Fiddler and apprentice fitter Colin Parry. *Cleve Jones*

box. My researches have revealed that the correct practice was to stop the train to uncouple the banker. However, it seems in order to save time that this little nicety was rarely indulged in! The final destination for this train was Hendre Sidings after shunting at Mold.

From my school windows at Broughton County Primary I was doubtless guilty of taking more interest in the passing trains than paying attention to my teachers. Thus between the years 1955 and 1960 I noted several things of interest that went beyond the norm on that long forgotten country branch line. One particular train that caught my junior eye was what my father called the 'gas train'. This '8F'-hauled ensemble could sometimes be espied on a Friday afternoon heading up* the branch and consisted of a number of flat wagons (about 20 or so) on which were mounted long creamy yellow tanks, possibly in longitudinal pairs. All very hush, hush it would be bound for the Ministry of Defence factory at Rhydymwyn which was about four miles beyond Mold. Some days later the same or similar entourage could be seen making its way back down the branch again. A derivative of phosgene or 'mustard gas' was made at Rhydymwyn up until 1945. Afterwards 'Cold War' materials were made or stored there, the branch trains were worked back to Warrington by Mold Junction shed. Engines other than '8Fs', Fowler '4Fs' were not generally assigned to the freight workings by my father, but there was a thrice-weekly 'Humpy'-worked out and back pick-up goods to Coed Talon, by then the furthest extremity of the old Mold-Brymbo branch. I once saw a Great Western Mogul run light engine through Broughton, apparently sneaking through to Hope Junction, this must have been out of gauge due to cylinder/platform clearance but I never heard of any mishaps. Also witnessed was a '5XP' 'Jubilee' working a down freight. My first ever sighting of a Metro-Cammell dmu set was in the summer of 1956 when the branch was first used for dmu driver training, and what a smart piece of kit that seemed like at the time.

The interesting thing about the curves commonly called the 'Circle' at Mold Junction is that apart from coming in useful for turning engines whenever the turntable was out of commission (not infrequently), and of course for their designated purpose of acting as a shunting link between the West and Mold ends, the outer curve (that nearest the centre of the triangle) which was of the greater radius was used for turning Pacific locomotives of over 65 ft in length, i.e. the Stanier 'Princess Royals' or 'Lizzies' and 'Duchesses'.

The turntable which nowadays has been transplanted and thoroughly rebuilt at a preserved railway (the Darley Dale Railway at Rowsley in the Peak District - *see photograph page 179*) was only 60 ft in length and could just about handle a 'Scot' with all wheels just on! I remember on summer weekends Chester shed used to get overloaded and engines would be sent down to 6B for stabling until the Monday morning. These locomotives often included a 'Big Lizzie' as my dad used to call all Stanier Pacifics, and to the best of my knowledge they didn't once put one on the floor whilst negotiating the triangle, a procedure undertaken amidst a cacophony of screaming flanges.

Thoughts of the West End remind of tales of that regular drivers dread, the sight test! All drivers and passed firemen had to undergo a stringent sight test. It was one of my father's more onerous tasks to carry out these tests personally.

* The correct terminology would be 'down' but it is easier to imagine the other way round as the down trains had to climb from Broughton to Pen-y-ffordd.

SHED STAFF — MOLD JUNCTION

J.E.(JACK) ROBINSON — SHEDMASTER

CLERKS OFFICE
MR BOWYER – CHIEF CLERK
BRIAN CADDY
ALAN ROBERTS

STORE KEEPERS
BOB PARRY
JOHN LARKIN
TOMMY DAVIES

BOILER WASHER
HARRY OVER

LEADING FITTERS
HAROLD EDWARDS
FRED HEWITT

FITTERS
BRON (BRONSKY) THE POLE
JACK FIDDLER
CHRIS GOFF
PAT GREENWOOD
LES MACY
BOB LEWIS
TED SANDERS
JACK ?

FIREDROPPERS
FRANK WHITE
BILL (TONKY) TONKS
FRANK (CAKE) JONES
BILL TOMS
JACK (GROOMY) GROOMS

BRICK ARCHER
LES NIXON

TIME KEEPERS
BOB WILLIAMS
TED McKAY (& STORES)
ALBERT (MARK SABER) SPROSTON

RUNNING SHIFT FOREMEN
TOM(PENSARN)JONES – LEADING
ERNIE WILLIAMS
BILL LUCAS

DEPUTIES
GEOFF EVANS
IDRIS MORRIS
OWEN HUGHES
WILF LIVERSAGE

For many years after Mold Junction shed's closure the 60 ft turntable remained *in situ* at the western end of the yard, it is seen here in 1979. The turntable was subsequently resited and beautifully restored by Peak Rail (*see page 179*). *Kevin Lane*

The routine was to take the candidate on foot (sometimes a lift on a westbound footplate could be gained) down to a point some 1,000 yards distant of the up home gantry which straddled the main line just on the down side of Mold Junction No. 3 box. The four track main line ran straight and level for almost a mile along the bottom edge of Hawarden airfield at this point and so provided an excellent testing ground for sighting signal movements on the said gantry. A plan of action would earlier have been agreed between my father and the signalman on duty, a flag raised by the tester indicating the instruction to pull off an agreed 'board' or 'peg'. The hapless footplate man would then have to say which signal was in the 'off' or 'on' position! This procedure would be repeated for several moves, perhaps some extra moves would be initiated by the passing of an up train. If all went well it was back to the shed for a welcome cup of hot tea. However, frequently it didn't go well and a man failed. The consequence of this was sometimes dire. Imagine the scenario where a senior top link driver is told there and then that he cannot go back on the on the main line! A bit like a professional truck driver of today losing his licence. Some men took it very badly indeed; some were offered the 'come down' of shunting or 'shed turning' duties. Either way it was a difficult task for my father to fail them but safety was rightly the rule of law. I used to pull his leg about his own sight, he always wore glasses for reading and close-up work. However, he had no difficulty seeing things over a mile away and so the sight tests were no problem to him.

As recorded by Max Dunn of Bangor shed:

On attaining the age of 50, 55 and 60 years every driver was given a medical sight test and if they failed to pass this test they were given a practical sight-test by the district motive power superintendent or locomotive shed master. This consisted of the correct reading of a standard semaphore signal on the lineside as follows:

The Shunters of Mold Junction

Driver Bill Dean eases carefully forward in the slate yard with 'Humpy' No. 47615. Note the number of wooden-bodied wagons still in evidence in this 1957 view.

Shunters Roy Kent (*left*) and Vic Allenby aboard No. 47650 on the West End shunt duties in the summer of 1956.

Driver Davy 'Where are we now?' Jones, pauses in the slate yard for a 'billy can' brew.

Mold Junction driver Arthur J. Rumsey (formerly of Abergavenny), on West End shunt duties, leans out of the cab of No. 47650. My dad used to kid me that the sand filler hole on the 'Humpy' was where the key went.

(All) Cleve Jones

Left: Some of Mold Junction's 'Likely Lads' grouped behind fitter Les Macey *circa* 1956. *From left to right*: passed cleaners Vic Challoner, Cyril Fletcher, Jack Lavener, Dai Jones and fitter's mate Roy Douggie.

Cleve Jones

Below left: Cleve Jones, seen here in 1956 as a 17-year-old passed cleaner posing next to Stanier 2-6-0 No. 42945, a long time stalwart of the shed. When Cleve was interviewed in 1954 for the job of cleaner, both his mother (who attended) and my father tried their hardest to put him off. Despite warnings of long hours of hard and dirty work for low pay he was determined to become an engine driver. Sadly, his ambition was to be beaten by progress, the shed closed while he was still a fireman and after a short and unhappy spell at Chester shed, before that too closed, he left the railway. We are to be eternally grateful that he had the foresight, like Max Dunn before him, to keep his camera handy on his daily working routine and so capture those precious workaday scenes often denied the enthusiast photographers of the day.

Cleve Jones

Driver Owen Hughes has just arrived at Green Lane, Saltney yard, *circa* mid-1950s with a loose-coupled trip working from Mold Junction, hence the van next to Stanier '8F' class 2-8-0 No. 48504 'borrowed' from Alsager shed. Note the top of the GWR water crane above the boiler. These workings were a daily occurrence that conversely saw the ex-GWR engines working into Mold Junction yard long before the closure of Chester (West) shed in April 1960.

Cleve Jones

Goods Train Departures From Mold Junction
(Mondays to Saturdays)

Extract of LM Western Lines working timetable between Llandudno Junction and Crewe
17th June to 15th September, 1957

Up direction					Down direction				
Dep.	To	Report.	Class	Remarks	Dep.	To	Report	Class	Remarks
am		No.			am		No.		
12.05	Walton Old Jn		H	MX	12.01	Caernarvon	59	H	MSX
1.00	Bushbury		H	SX	12.23	Caernarvon	59	H	SO
1.12	Bushbury		H		1.05	Menai Bridge	53	H	MO
1.30	Weaste Jn		H	MX	1.15	Llandudno Jn	44	H	SO
2.06	Birkenhead	55	J	MX	1.40	Llandudno Jn	44	H	SX
2.20	Garston		J	MO Q E	2.00	Holyhead	74	H	MO
2.57	Rugby Midland		E	SX	3.05	Holyhead	74	H	SO
3.22	Whitchurch		H	MO	3.30	Menai Bridge	21	K	MO
3.25	Rugby Midland		E	SO	4.36	Mostyn		J	SO
3.50	Guide Bridge		H	MX	5.15	Denbigh	41	H	
3.55	Crewe		H	MO	6.00	Mold	40	H	SX
4.40	Crewe		H	MX	6.35	Menai Bridge		H	MX
4.45	Rowsley		H	MO	7.00	Holywell Jn	56	J	SX
4.50	Saltney		K	SO	7.18	Central Electricity		J	
5.05	Port Sunlight		F	MX		Authority Marsh Sidings			
5.10	Crewe		H	SO	7.25	Muspratt's Sidings		K	
5.15	Port Sunlight		F	MO	8.50	Llandudno Jn	32	H	MO
5.50	Guide Bridge		H	MO	9.23	Denbigh	62	H	
6.05	Crewe		H	MSX	10.45	Hendre Siding	45	K	SX
6.05	Crewe		H	MO	10.55	Hendre Siding	45	K	SO
10.35	Chester		K	SX					
11.30	Saltney		K	SX					
pm					pm				
12.50	Alsager		F	SX	12.45	Llandudno Jn	23	J	SX
3.20	Saltney		K	SX	1.45	Muspratt's Sidings	47	H	SX
6.00	Normacot Jn		F	SX E	2.45	Central Electricity	44	K	SX
6.15	Port Sunlight		J	SX		Authority Marsh Sidings			
7.12	Crewe		H	SX	3.35	Holyhead		H	SX
7.18	Ellesmere Port	43	H	SO	4.00	Central Electricity	44	K	SO
7.35	Normacot Jn		F	SO E		Authority Marsh Sidings			
8.25	Brook Lane, Chester		K	SO	5.35	Holywell Jn		H	SO
8.50	Runcorn		F	SX E	6.25	Holyhead		H	SX
9.10	York		E	SO	7.10	Holyhead	5	J	SO
9.30	Cheadle Jn		F	SX E	7.15	Bangor	50	J	MSX
10.20	Copley Hill		H	SO	7.50	Llandudno Jn	64	J	SX
10.20	Copley Hill		H	SX	7.50	Llandudno Jn	23	K	SX
10.45	Crewe		E	SO	10.55	Menai Bridge	52	H	SX
11.05	Chester	22	K	SX					
11.05	Walton Old Jn		H	SO					
11.30	Ellesmere Port	39	H	SX					
11.35	Edge Hill		F	SX					
11.55	Edge Hill		H	FSX					

Key
E - Empties, FSX - Fridays & Saturdays excepted, MO - Mondays only,
MSX - Mondays & Saturdays excepted, MX - Mondays excepted, Q - Runs when required,
SO - Saturdays only, SX - Saturdays excepted.

Courtesy of R. Carvell

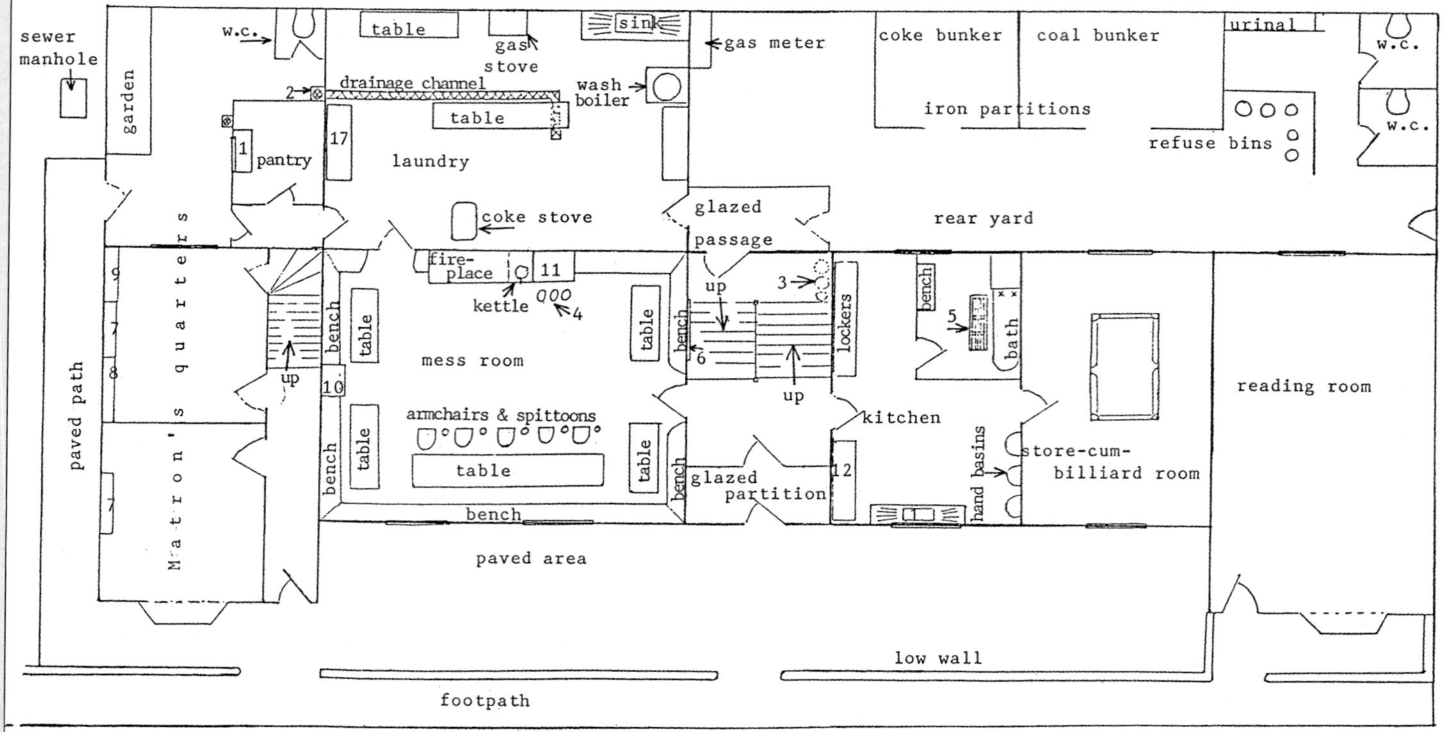

Ground Floor

The barracks at Mold Junction.

D. Goodwin

w.c.
urinal
w.c.
coal bunker
refuse bins
coke bunker
iron partitions
reading room
store-cum-billiard room
hand basins
bath
bench
5
lockers
kitchen
12
up
gas meter
glazed passage
up
3
up
6
bench
table
bench
table
glazed partition
low wall
sink
wash boiler
coke stove
gas stove
table
drainage channel
laundry
17
fireplace
11
kettle
4
mess room
armchairs & spittoons
table
bench
paved area
footpath
table
bench
10
up
table
bench
pantry
2
1
w.c.
Matron's quarters
garden
sewer manhole
paved path

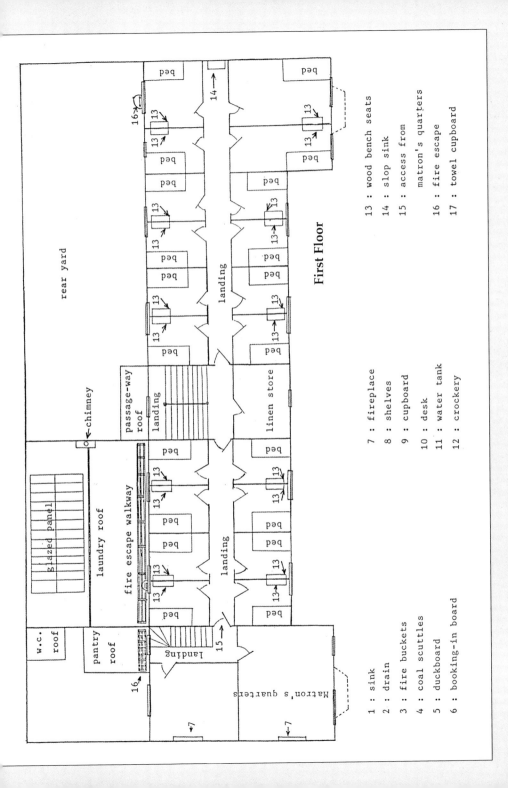

First Floor

1 : sink
2 : drain
3 : fire buckets
4 : coal scuttles
5 : duckboard
6 : booking-in board

7 : fireplace
8 : shelves
9 : cupboard
10 : desk
11 : water tank
12 : crockery

13 : wood bench seats
14 : slop sink
15 : access from
    matron's quarters
16 : fire escape
17 : towel cupboard

1,000 yards both eyes together 500 yards each eye separately	Main line test
400 yards both eyes together 200 yards each eye separately	Shunting test

This practical sight-test had to be repeated every two years after the age of 60.

The area in the centre of the triangle was occupied by four sidings belonging to the Permanent Way Department which also had a crane- and rail-served store at their disposal. Back across the main line alongside the slate yard shunting neck was sited the yardmaster's office, or the home of the 'Traffic people' as enginemen were sometimes known to call them disparagingly. There was always a gulf of animosity twixt the two departments which I think was borne out of 'Traffics' regular insistence on the motive power depot attending to yard breakdowns promptly, breakdowns invariably caused by 'Traffic' in the first place!

When you add the non-railway appendages of the hostel, school, shops and houses of the Mold Junction 'spread' to the railway items already mentioned, you begin to realize just what an empire 'Spike Island' was. For my father's part, of course, he had no jurisdiction whatsoever over the Traffic Dept, but the hostel did fall under his control and for many years he chaired the monthly Locomotive Department Committee (or LDC) meetings in the mess room at that establishment, known affectionately to its one-night residents as either the 'Barracks' or the 'Hostel'. Maybe this extra responsibility plus the growing importance of Mold Junction had something to do with it, but I like to believe it was for more profound reasons that one evening in 1957 he arrived home 'cock a hoop' to announce that he had been promoted to special 'A' status. This involved a salary rise, which was by now paid in cash fortnightly on a Thursday and elevated his status to that of shed masters at larger depots such as Birkenhead. It also involved an increase in personal and family travel benefits. The latter was, I think, the one part of his remuneration that was worth its weight in gold as it enabled the relatively poor families of railwaymen to have holidays away from home, something which today I regard as one of the most precious of my childhood experiences.

In those days the 'perk' as we would term it today consisted of about four free second class passes a year on the 'Home' London Midland Region (LMR) with, I think, two further ones on a 'Foreign' region. The privilege extended to all members of the family under 16 years of age (or those still in full time education). However, added to the free passes came the invaluable use of limitless Privilege Tickets (or 'PTs') which were in effect a small pack of tear off slips that my father carried that entitled him and his entourage to second class quarter rate fares on any journey (i.e. 25 per cent of the public rate). Excellent for getting about when one was 'encamped' at the chosen holiday destination. It must be appreciated that in those pre-Beeching days most worthwhile holiday destinations, especially the seaside ones, could be reached by rail and many were in central positions that allowed daily excursions along local branch lines to an undoubted wealth of fine destinations.

Chapter Eight

A Miscellany

Mentioned earlier was our family move from Llandudno Junction to a new council house at Broughton in April 1954. The terraced house was on a relatively large estate overlooking a green in the front with open fields to the rear. Whilst there was a pre-disposition for most of the houses to be occupied by employees from the local De Havilland aircraft factory, it is interesting to note that in amongst this majority was a not inconsiderable number of railwaymen and their families. In our terrace of nine houses there were no less than three railway families comprising Tom Lloyd, a signalman at Broughton & Bretton, Vic Allenby a shunter at Mold Junction yard and ourselves. In an opposite house resided Mick Mayfield who worked in the water softening plant at Chester. At the other end of the estate lived Emrys Williams, a 6B driver (who gave considerable help when researching this book), who although about 20 years younger than my father complained that he always had a job keeping up with him when they cycled to the shed together! If there was one common thing that made a railwayman's house stand out from the rest, it was the immaculate garden with an even more well kept vegetable garden to the rear. You see by comparison with others, railway wages were low and it was important to take advantage of the opportunities a garden provided to ease the family food bill. I remember one Sunday evening as we were walking home from church with John Williams (a local crossing keeper) and his wife, John overheard the two ladies extolling the advantages of owning a washing machine which most of the 'De Havilland' wives had by then (mid-1950s) acquired. John loudly exclaimed to my dad, 'We've already got a washing machine - she's walking in front of us!'

One notable 'De Havilland' next door neighbour in the mid-1950s was Frank Costin and his family. Being an engineer Frank got on famously with my father as not only did he hail from north London, where he had served his apprenticeship with the General Aircraft Co. at Hanworth, he being a senior aerodynamicist had quite a lot to say about locomotive streamlining. One Saturday afternoon I went next door to find Frank and my father deeply engrossed with sheets of calculations and sketch drawings all over the dining room table and floor. Using their joint knowledge and expertise they were engaged in an exercise to find at what theoretical speed, with the extra weight and less drag, would the streamlining of a Stanier 'Duchess' start to have an advantageous effect. I think Frank concluded that at less than about 120 mph it was a waste of time! In fact it only added to the coal and water consumption, and this was echoed somewhat by Stanier's attitude to the whole business of streamlining. Frank moved from aviation to motor racing where he was well known for his trend setting designs for Lotus and Vanwall. Renowned for his work in glass fibre and wood, he was able to squeeze prodigious performances from his 'slippery' car body shapes with minimal size engines and he later founded with Gem Marsh the Marcos Car Co. Sadly, he died of cancer aged 74 in 1995.

My mother recovered considerably from her wartime leg injury whilst living at Broughton, so much so that in 1957 she decided that whilst finding a job to ease the family's finances wasn't really feasible, taking in a lodger would be. She contacted the personnel dept at De Havilland's who in turn sent along a young apprentice called Michael Smith whose family lived in Crewe. Michael echoed my own future in that he was an engineering apprentice and at that time was busy studying for his HNC and each evening he would set about the mounds of homework that studying on a day release course generates. Well not, that is, before I had collared him each night to assist with my own nightly homework which at that tender age consisted of a practice run for the weekly Friday morning spelling test. This done, I would 'insist' that he help out with my latest Meccano construction project. Poor lad, when I asked him what he would do if I had a No. 10 set, his answer came in one word - 'Leave!' The first thing my mother indulged in with her new found wealth was to replace her beloved 'Rurr d' Durr Durr'* with a reconditioned electric vacuum cleaner of the cylinder variety, luxury indeed!

Michael never really got on with our cat so after about 18 months of punishment from both me and it he finally did leave. In due course he was replaced by another much more senior De Havilland's employee, a machine shop supervisor by the name of Sam Wood, an ardent golfing bachelor who hailed from Oldham in Lancashire. Unfortunately for my father neither of these characters had any interest in railways, never mind steam engines that by then were largely considered to be 'old hat' anyway.

Transports of Delight!

Not long after our move to Broughton in 1954 my parents (not me!) decided that I had a problem with my feet, i.e. they were flat! Our local GP referred me for specialist treatment as an outpatient at the (of all places) Royal Southern Hospital in Liverpool. Following this referral I spent the next 10 years travelling, at first every six months and after a few years every 12 months, to this medical establishment with my mother. One could reasonably argue that I witnessed the most profound changes in that city's transport system over those years. In the beginning (1955), the journey began at Broughton & Bretton station for the short four mile journey to Chester. Here we would board a Western Region express for the final stage of its long journey from Paddington to Birkenhead. Motive power would invariably be an ex-Great Western '51XX' Prairie tank of either Chester (84K) or Birkenhead (6C) sheds. I seemed to recall a mass of sidings alongside the Nuclear Fuels plant at Capenhurst, that place was huge and shrouded in secrecy. Many years later, visiting the place in the mid-1960s as an apprentice, I found out why. During the 1950s it ranked alongside Aldermaston in importance, as most of the material for the MOD's nuclear armaments was refined there in a series of massive centrifuges. Subsequently it was also revealed that it was a prime Cold War target for our red star 'friends'; well that would have wiped Cheshire and Merseyside off the map if hostilities had ever resulted!

---

* A pre-war friction driven upright contraption that made a noise resembling the above description when pushed back and forth across a carpet. She always had a way with words!

On alighting at Rock Ferry we would board what to me then seemed like a monstrosity, a vintage Mersey Railway electric set by then sporting a sickly mid-green livery adorned with a 'Ferret & Dartboard' motif. I think it was on one of these subterranean trips that I espied my first black man! Of course on arrival in Liverpool I saw many more and my mother explained that they were 'stokers off the ships!' Having rock and rolled our way beneath the Mersey in fine Edwardian style we emerged into the concourse of Liverpool's Central station which, in those days of course, was a hive of steamy activity. Out onto the bustling street and we were greeted by the clank and screech of trams making their way up and down Church Street to and from the Pier Head. I never got a ride on a 'Green Goddess' tramcar, despite my mum suggesting we take a trip to Pier Head and back, for some forgotten and unfortunate reason it just didn't happen. There would be time to look at the shops and invariably (for my mum at least) the likes of Lewis's, Blackler's or George Henry Lee's beckoned. After a brief lunch in one of these establishments it was then a short walk to Renshaw Street to catch the bus for the mile or so to the top of Hill Street amid the bombed-out air raid ruins that typified so much of post-war Liverpool. We then crossed the road for (what seemed to me) the long walk down to the Royal Southern. As that place was neared so came the strains of the sound of electric trains humming and clattering along - yes the Liverpool Overhead Railway! This fine linear edifice (for that is what it was) was sandwiched twixt the hospital and the massive Brunswick dock grain silos. I shall never forget the sights and echoing sounds of those stumpy old brown three-car sets rattling along their elevated tracks above the docks at that place. If one was lucky a red Tate & Lyle Sentinel steam wagon, possibly pulling a trailer, might also be seen climbing up Hill Street from the Brunswick Dock. As I remember, they climbed the relatively steep hill with exemplary ease!

Our return to Chester was usually our outward journey in reverse, but just occasionally we sampled the Mersey ferry to Woodside. I do have a firm memory that the Prairie tanks always seemed to work bunker first back to Chester.

Strangely in those far off days the Birkenhead Joint seemed more Great Western than LMS, probably because it was the apex of the former's system and a very important outlet for their export traffic etc. Notwithstanding this, once one left Chester there was very little in the way of Great Western lineside artifacts to be seen. All signalling was ex-LMS (LNWR) and station architecture seemed indifferent. Apparently when the line was constructed the LNWR came up with a much cheaper tender for the signalling and so, unlike the Shrewsbury-Hereford joint line, where a right mixture held sway, the Great Western agreed, for cost reasons, to let the LNWR get on with it! I have a lasting memory of witnessing, in the summer of 1957, a gleaming (clearly ex-works) black ex-Great Western '28XX' 2-8-0 running at 'full pelt' through Rock Ferry station en route for Birkenhead. I don't think I have ever witnessed a light engine running so fast before or since!

For one trip only my father accompanied us, I think it was in 1963 but I can't be certain. On arrival we split up for an hour with my mum heading for her favourite shopping haunts whilst my dad promised to show me what a 'proper'

LNWR station was like. This, of course, turned out to be Lime Street which to this day remains the grandest ex-'Premier Line' station still in existence and possibly one of the grandest terminii in the country. In those days it had only recently been electrified and was populated by the pale blue 25Kv 'E3000' class Bo-Bo electrics which at that time were fitted with large mercury arc rectifiers. By then these locomotives had displaced the Edge Hill 'Princess' Pacifics although many of the non-electrified routes were still steam-worked.

By the time of my last visit to the Royal Southern in the summer of 1965 so many things had changed on the transport scene that, on reflection, it was a case of being in Liverpool 'just in time' to witness the passing of so much of the city's rich transport heritage.

Meccano

I have made passing reference to my junior activities with that most well-known of boys' construction sets. My dad had given me as a five-year-old (Christmas 1953) a No. 2 set to see if it would strike a chord of interest. Well it did and over a period another five years or so I acquired a couple more sets leading to a No. 4 set; this combined with the others enabled a fair selection of different things to be built. When at the age of about 10 I started to take an interest in how a locomotive worked he set about making up a demonstration set of Walchaerts valve gear. This involved modifying some of the parts in order to get a working representation of an expansion link, but what did result was a fully working set with a reversible motion via a screw reverser. On another occasion, as a result of my questioning how the Mold Junction coaling plant worked, he built for me a model with a working wagon hoist and a 'Jiggler'.*

Model Making

My father had a long-held ambition that when he retired he would purchase a second-hand Myford lathe and set about making a working steam model of the much-heralded BR Standard '8P' Pacific No. 71000 *Duke of Gloucester*. From the summer of 1954 he began collecting a series of model engineering magazines that had a running article devoted to the construction of a working three-cylinder 'O' gauge steam model of this particular locomotive. Now I think it would have been much easier in one of the larger scales but that is purely hypothetical thinking as he never got to make his model. However, my own interests in model making, like so many of my youthful contemporaries, were fired up by those cheap and cheerful plastic 'Airfix' kits. Two shillings would get you a 'Spitfire' and my very first effort was a 'Gloster Gladiator', but I had to rely on my dad to put the biplane together as my skills were not yet well enough fostered. Despite giving up on a 'Westland Whirlwind' helicopter I managed to successfully put together an 'ME109' to go into battle with my 'Spit'

* The horizontally oscillating open-ended bucket device that regulated the volume of coal being dropped into a tender.

atop our post-war 'Ultra' wireless set. So when in 1959 there came the famous 'Kitmaster' range of 'OO' gauge plastic locomotive kits you can imagine how my enthusiasm was boosted!

First off that summer was the 'Lanky' 0-4-0 Pug retailing at 4s. 6d., still in my collection today. Again my dad had to attend to the finer parts such as the cross heads and motion. The following Christmas brought the Stanier 'Duchess' Pacific and so on until my mum realized that even at 10s. 6d. they were remarkably good value and so became a major armament in her agenda to cure me of the wretched childhood habit of nailbiting! It worked and by the time I was cured I had a bookcase full of models made over a period of about three years, fittingly the last one built was No. 92220 *Evening Star*. Well plastic kits are alright to look at but they don't go do they? (or at least they didn't in those days). So in 1963 I saved my Christmas money and went out and bought a rare 'K's' whitemetal kit complete with wheels and motor. This absolutely delighted my dad as it was the LNWR 0-6-2 'Coal Tank' (or 'Gadget' as he always called them). So that Christmas our first evenings in our (new) Curzon Park abode were spent labouring away on this little engine. 'It's not got any brakes' said my dad: 'We'll soon cure that, the originals were wooden blocks you know'. He then set about carving up one of his old Briars, the inner diameter of the bowl was just about right to match the outside tyre diameter on the driving wheels!

When later in 1964 Max Dunn visited us, not long after completing the rescue of '1054' (*see Chapter Ten*), I pronounced that I had got something to show him. My model wasn't 1054 but it did then have an LNWR number plate on the tank side, 'Gosh I, I, I, don't believe it!', he stammered as he picked it up, 'Is it 1054?'

The Buckley Railway

In September 1960 I commenced at Hawarden Grammar School and from the early summer of 1961 I have fond memories of travelling with my class on a rickety old Bedford bus up to Buckley Baths for weekly Friday morning swimming lessons. About halfway up the hill to Buckley from Ewloe the road passed under what seemed to me an equally rickety old (single track) railway bridge. Now having made this journey a number of times the presence of this edifice began to fascinate me. What line could this be? It certainly wasn't the Wrexham-Shotton line as this passed through a station in Hawarden* village and it certainly didn't connect to the disused line† that ran under the A55 past the school tuck shop near the start of Ewloe village. Although the line appeared to run past a number of still extant brickworks there never seemed (to me at least) to be any moving or standing traffic on it. I questioned my dad about it and he suggested that when I got the chance I should ask Max who had written a book about lines in that area. This in due course I did. 'It's the Buckley Railway old chap', came his reply, 'part of the old Wrexham, Mold & Connah's Quay, it's very interesting so try to take a good look at it, it runs from Buckley Junction down to Connah's Quay'.

* Pronounced 'Harden'.
† Remains of the old Aston Hall Tramway that connected coal mines near Buckley to wharfs on the Dee.

Well a couple of years later, in March 1963 to be precise, I did just that. One of my school pals who was also interested in railways invited me up to his abode which just happened to be in a small copse almost alongside the line near the Castle Brickworks between Buckley and Northop Hall (by then the terminus of the line). It was a chilly but dry Saturday morning and I cycled up to his house from Broughton, a distance of about six miles, uphill all the way!

To begin with we joined the line at a level crossing close to his home, this was quaint insomuch as adjacent to it was a crossing keeper's cottage. This, I believe, was called 'Mary's Cottage' after the one time lady keeper and the hand-operated gates were guarded by lattice post signals worked by heel brackets mounted at the base of each gate. We walked on from here in the northerly direction of Connah's Quay and soon passed over a wooden trestle bridge that carried the line over the busy A55 road that was in a gully below. The going then got exceedingly muddy as there was a steep-sided cutting leading to an overbridge and thence into a coal yard consisting of a truncated loop that was in effect the Northop Hall terminus.

We had not long been at that point when we spotted a plume of steam rising up from the woods from where we had come. 'It's a train', my pal shouted and sure enough out of the cutting chuffed a pannier tank with a couple of coal wagons and a brake van behind! We ran back to meet the ensemble which by now had stopped before entering the sidings. It was one of Croes Newydd's '16XX' panniers and they were about to do something that I had never witnessed before, a spot of 'fly shunting'. As the loop had been taken out at the far end of the yard, and therefore the engine could not run around its train, it was necessary to 'fly shunt' the brake van into a spur siding so that it could be towed rather than propelled back to Buckley on the return trip. Probably as there were other wagons waiting to be picked up full from brickworks back up the line. So having stopped, the guard climbed down from his van with a shunter's pole and gently the engine started forward. When a speed of about 3-4 mph had been gained the engine brake was partially applied allowing the coupling twixt the van and rearmost wagon to slacken. The guard lifted off the shackle and this done he signalled the driver to accelerate away leaving the brake van rolling forward at a slow walking pace, the guard then ran forward to throw the point leading to the spur, as the van passed him he jumped aboard and applied the brake when it had entered the spur and fully cleared the points. By this time the engine had reversed the two wagons into the coal yard siding where they were left with brakes pinned down. We then set off back up the line on foot so that we could see the engine and brake van returning 'at speed'!

We had got as far as the muddy cutting when there was a loud shriek from that Great Western whistle, he was catching us up fast and we had to break into a run to get out of the cutting as the sides were too slippery to present an escape route! Just then the driver opened up the cylinder cocks (a classic way to shift straying animals!) and we jumped clear onto flat ground by the road bridge. In those days despite my father's teaching, my knowledge of a locomotive's anatomy wasn't as good as I thought it was. When I described my experiences later to him I said that the driver had opened the 'snifting valves'; he nearly went crazy with me!

That afternoon after lunch at my pal's home we set off in the opposite direction to Buckley. Here we passed a number of operational brickworks that had their own sidings with loading platforms etc. The first was Castle brickworks then came Gibsons and over the Ewloe road bridge we came to the Ewloe Barn works, by then owned by General Refractories and making highly complex gas fire grills etc. This pattern of things carried on all the way through the lower outskirts of Buckley, one brickworks after another, I lost count of how many private sidings we passed before we arrived at Buckley Junction where the line connected to the ex-Great Central Railway double track line from Wrexham to Shotton and beyond. To think that today, in most places at least, no trace of that old branch line or the brickworks and collieries it served remains.

I recall that we took a short trip on a dmu down to Hawarden Bridge Halt (for Summers Steelworks), where whilst waiting for a return train I espied an ex-Great Western '56XX' 0-6-2T shunting by Dee Marsh signal box some 500 yards further down the line. On alighting at Buckley Junction we decided to hang around in case the '56XX' should be coming back up to Wrexham. We were soon to be rewarded as the sounds of an engine working really hard came into earshot. It was that 0-6-2T, an ideal engine for the short but gruelling climb up Hawarden bank. As the train passed us at about 15 mph amid an absolute cacophony of exhaust and blowing safety valves it seemed like the fire was just about being lifted off the grate judging by the shower that was descending on us - what an experience! Many times whilst at school we would spend our lunch breaks watching the '56XX' and '57XX' panniers struggling up the 1 in 50 of the Hawarden bank with Dee Marsh-Croes Newydd freights. Towards 1965 the ex-GWR '38XX' and ex-LMS Stanier '8F' 2-8-0s became more common on the heavier workings as by that time both classes were shedded at Wrexham.

Buckley Junction, view looking north *circa* 1952.   *J.M. Dunn*

The author's first footplate experience. Margate, August 1952. *Author's Collection*

Due to the short platform length at Birkenhead Woodside, two coaches had to be removed from the return working of a Birkenhead-Margate special at Chester. They will be stored until the next day when they will be re-attached for the outward trip. On 8th September, 1954 Oxford shed's 'Hall' class 4-6-0 No. 4938 *Liddington Hall* shunts the ex-Southern Railway stock around the Chester West cutting past No. 4 signal box. *S.D. Wainwright*

Chapter Nine

Holidays and High Days

Well let's start at the beginning: faint as the memories of over 50 years ago are to me now, they still possess those certain ingredients that keep them firmly glued in the mind's eye ... steam engines and a train journey!

Almost every year of my childhood was greatly enlightened by the annual summer holiday. Being born later on in my parent's marriage I was to enjoy the privileges, unheard of before the war, of this luxury. Luxury was the word to this infant railway lover, second only to the beach and his bucket and spade, the journey to the destination was the highlight of his sabbatical.

The first holiday of which I have any recollection was the one taken in August 1952. The destination was Margate on the Isle of Thanet in Kent. I have a clear memory of the tapered-boiler 'Scot' arriving at platform 1 at Llandudno Junction, its smoke box door adorned with a 'reporting number', a vague recollection of the endless journey to Euston that followed, but no recollection at all of the subsequent journey from Victoria to Margate (I was probably asleep!). Margate was our destination primarily because it was the home of my father's, by now widowed, stepmother. A crusty old girl known to my sister and I as plain Grandma! (That's original isn't it?)

The following year 1953 stands out more clearly. We again visited a seaside town where my father's younger sister Marjorie had a ladies hairdresser's shop. The town was none other that that 'Jewel in the English Riviera' Torquay. This time the journey was much more interesting as it was broken first at Chester where the young 'Robbo' got his first experience of the sights and sounds of a Great Western engine. Like all children of my generation who had the vaguest interest in railways, the GWR engines made an immediate and lasting impression with their cleanliness and copper/brass adornments. Even the sounds were so different from the LMS engines, the 'stit...stit...stit' of their vacuum pumps, the 'whooshing' noise of their injectors singing, etc. All this combined to start yours truly off on a love affair that still goes on today. I might tell you that my infatuation didn't half annoy my dad in his later years, but more of that anon!

My first reaction as the train left Chester was to ask why we were going back to the 'Junction', this amused my dad no end who just played along with my fear that we weren't going on holiday after all. This fear being dispelled of course as soon as the train turned due south at Saltney Junction. Few other things stand out in my memory like the scariness of going through the Severn Tunnel, again heightened by my dad who really liked to tease me. I distinctly remember the sight of a 'Hall' or similar class of locomotive slipping like mad in a shed yard, probably Bristol Bath Road. Other railway memories include a trip from Torquay to Plymouth behind a '51XX' class Prairie tank. Of course Plymouth in those days was a bombed-out shell very similar to Liverpool in appearances!

The following year, 1954, we moved house to Broughton and so did without a holiday as such. My grandmother's house at the Junction stood in as it later always did for makeshift 'hols' with days out at Deganwy beach as a typical way of relaxing. The journey to that estuary beach, of course, invariably taken by train from the Junction station. Today's kids jet off to the 'Med' with monotonous regularity and I'm sure they don't enjoy themselves half as much as we did then.

The next year 1955 it was back to Margate again, but this time with a difference. Lots of people may have heard about, or indeed, remember the Birkenhead-Ramsgate specials. Well I can claim to go one better than that, I've travelled on one ... all the way from Chester to Margate. Imagine boarding green-liveried ex-Southern stock in platform 2 of Chester station! That journey seemed to take a lifetime, it started with my dad and I sitting on our suitcases in the corridor of an absolutely packed train, I distinctly remember our engine, one of the ubiquitous 'Halls', labouring away up Gresford bank with the rain coming down the carriage windows. Well how else did you start a holiday in Blighty in those days? Anyway after Shrewsbury the crowding eased and we were able to join the rest of the party in a compartment. The tunnels around Snow Hill, Birmingham stick in my mind's eye as did those GWR railcars we termed 'Flying Bananas', they were seen in profusion around Reading. If my memory serves me right we had the same engine on all the way down to Redhill, deep in Southern territory. There I distinctly remember our gleaming 'Hall' coming off the train and being replaced by one of those 'boxy looking Southern objects' as my dad was wont to call a Bulleid Pacific.* Shortly after leaving Redhill in the reverse direction from which we had entered I remember catching sight, for the first time, of a train of Pullman stock redolent in its cream and brown livery. The 'Hall' was probably a Chester (84K) engine and would be diagrammed† to work back in that direction with the same train the following morning and the same crew as the outward working. I think, in those days, Chester crews worked the train back home from Oxford after a lodging turn. Anyway it was one of those interesting inter-regional trains that echoed the 'Sunny South Express' of the former London & North Western/London, Brighton & South Coast railways.

The June 1956 Whitsuntide school half-term break saw me once more down at the Junction for a few days. Nothing special in this apart from it being the event of my first ever trip on a diesel train! In March of that year a fleet of brand new 'Derby Lightweights' had displaced the steam passenger workings on the Blaenau Ffestiniog branch. These early dmus probably saved the branch from entering the history books. Their clean open airiness and observation car coach ends had a remarkable effect on passenger receipts and the publicity department at the Junction put on a series of special Sunday afternoon workings as far as Betws-y-Coed for a short while in the summer months only. My Aunt Sophie took me on one of these trips and I have lingering recollections of her being 'chatted up' by the driver who, of course, knew her!

July 1956 brought with it my first and only (to date) experience of seasickness with a trip to 'Mona's Isle'. The journey again began behind an ex-GWR '41XX' prairie tank, this time of short duration, from Chester to Birkenhead Woodside, there to take the 'Ferry 'cross the Mersey' to the Isle of Man Steam Packet ship

---

* Generally referred to as 'Spam Cans' by the trainspotting fraternity.
† Normally engines were changed at Oxford on both outward and return journeys.

Lady of Mann. I think at the time she was the packet's flagship, certainly she was a vintage vessel with an abundance of wood panelling, etc. All went well until my dad bought me a small tub of ice cream, there was a good swell going! It goes without saying that I was smitten by the Manx railways: my first ever journey on a narrow gauge train was from Douglas to Peel. I can hear my dad saying the words now, 'You can get half crowns between these dammed rail joints!' Well the joints were a bit wide and the speed at which the trains ran exemplified this, the 'clickety, click' had become 'clunkety clack'. All in a day's sheer enjoyment for this chap whose only disappointment was that the locomotives all looked the same! A journey to Port Erin soon followed and to this day my one regret is that we never made a journey down the Ramsey line from St John's. Having been brought up amongst the trams at Llandudno and Colwyn Bay, there didn't seem anything special about the Manx Electric Railway. But I do remember enjoying a trip to Laxey on an open 'toast rack', whereupon we boarded the sinister confines of a Snaefell car for a trip to the summit.

Before we move on to the main holiday event of 1957 there is another experience that is worth relating that happened in early May of that year. My big sister Ann had got married in the March to a certain young fellow called Ronald Woodward from Ashton Hayes (a small village about six miles to the east of Chester). Ron, as he was always called, was the only son of Herbert and Margaret Woodward and Herbert was a signalman at Mouldsworth Junction on the Cheshire Lines route between Manchester Central and Chester Northgate. Herbert was quite a character who spoke with a pronounced Cheshire accent and, when relating a tale, invariably began most sentences with the words 'Any road up …'! This might be construed as somewhat 'dodgy' for a signalman of his long standing, but the fact that he always wore a belt with his braces did something to temper any doubts one might have about his 'reliability in office'. I digress, the main point of the story was that, having now married, our couple planned to emigrate to Canada, Toronto to be more precise, and the means of emigration was by Cunard steamship from Liverpool. The day of sailing was, if my memory serves me correctly, 6th May or thereabouts. The plan was that the mothers would say their goodbyes at Chester (General) station and Herbert, dad and myself would accompany the intrepid couple to Liverpool and see them aboard the ship.

Well Ron had a rather nice black post-war Ford 'Prefect' of which he was justifiably proud and somewhat loath to get rid of. It would be an understatement to say that he was cutting it a bit fine when he dropped us off at the station entrance and then drove the car around to the Brook Street Auctions. There he sold it before returning on foot to meet up with us in the station café which was then adjacent to platform 2. My mum was 'on pins' and we had already seen the departure of one Woodside train before he showed up beaming with the success of his hurried transaction. With time to spare before the departure of the next train (a local from the bay platform 3), we sauntered down to the end of the platform and witnessed an ex-GWR 'Castle' (that had brought in the ex-Paddington train that we had missed) backing slowly down to the colour light signal at the end of platform 2. 'Well go on then, tell us what's

An ex-LNER class 'O4/3' 2-8-0 No. 63713 blasts through Mouldsworth in April 1959 with a Dee Marsh-Northwich mixed freight. Note the Cheshire Lines Committee signals.   *Norman Jones*

Signalman Herbert Woodward hands the Helsby branch token to the driver of 'O1' class 2-8-0 No. 64824 passing slowly through Mouldsworth in April 1959. Timber can be seen in the leading wagons.   *Norman Jones*

wrong with that one!', exclaimed Ron to my dad, with a cheeky grin. Inevitably the 'Castle' (Earl of something or other) was pristine in her green livery and dad just shrugged his shoulders and said, 'It's one of theirs ... seems alright to me!' Little did he know then that in just over three years time that class of locomotive and her sisters would become just another of his problems and no longer 'one of theirs'! Notwithstanding that, of all the Great Western engines that he dealt with in later years he had a healthy respect for the four-cylinder 'Castles' with their inside Walchaerts valve gear and built in micrometer valve adjusters. He considered a good one to be a veritable 'Rolls Royce' amongst locomotives, a testimony indeed from an LMS man! An ex-LMS driver who had experienced the 'Castles' might not be so complimentary though, as more than likely he would be reminded of the multitudinous motion oiling points that the locomotive possessed, something in excess of 90 I believe! Our departure amongst tearful farewells from the women folk eventually came and in due course we arrived at Birkenhead Woodside. As we emerged from the ramp onto the ferry pier we got our first view of that splendid Cunard vessel *Carinthia*, which was moored along the main landing stage across the River Mersey at Liverpool.

For those interested in shipping, the *Carinthia* was completed the previous year at John Brown's on Clydeside having been launched in December 1955. She was one of four 22,000 tonners built by Cunard for its Canadian services and she had the distinction of being named by Princess Margaret. Her sister ships were *Saxonia*, *Invernia* and *Sylvania* all built between 1954 and 1957. Each one had a relatively shallow draught and short masts enabling them to sail under the bridges in the St Lawrence River. To a distinctly impressionable eight-year-old boy that ship was just about the most fantastic thing he had ever seen. Once we alighted from the ferry and were able to walk along the dockside to the boarding and departure buildings it seemed like I was observing a veritable monster that arose out of the water and fairly touched the clouds above! From within a busy and crowded departure shed we said our final farewells and then we retreated once more onto the dockside to await the ship's grand departure to the New World, or at least to the middle of the Mersey to wait on the incoming tide that night! After a short while our couple emerged on the upper port deck to wave goodbye and then it happened completely without warning ... the ship's hooter sounded a long deafening burst! I'm told by the so-called experts that my deafness is hereditary, but if you ask me it could well have been started by that incredible cacophony. By my reckoning you could have heard it way up the coast in Blackpool! That was just the first of several blasts emitted before the beast was cast off and made its manoeuvre into mid-river just as it was going dark.

The ensuing journey home that evening I remember well if only for its trivia. Firstly there was the walk to James Street station beneath the ghostly remains of the by now defunct 'Dockers Umbrella', then came the long descent of the stairs down to the dark and dank platform at James Street. Finally, I distinctly remember, whilst waiting for our Chester train on platform 1 (now long gone) at Rock Ferry station, Herbert remarked on the brightness of the signal lamp in the up starter. His remarks went something like this. 'By eck that's a bright'un, it

A westbound freight train in Delamere Forest headed by an unidentifed ex-LNER 2-8-0. This is
the section where Herbert Woodward 'lost a train' going in the opposite direction.

Norman Jones

Herbert Woodward with his trusty BSA motorcycle at the end of the platform at Mouldsworth.
The line to the left is for Chester and that to the right for Helsby.   *Norman Jones*

must be electric!' To which my Dad replied, 'No I don't think so, the spectacle has probably recently been cleaned!' Herbert then replied with a sigh, 'Aye appen'. Well our three-coach stopper shortly pulled in behind an Ivatt 'tanky' and off we went back to Chester. Ten years were to elapse before I found myself regularly using that same Rock Ferry platform again late every Saturday night as I made my way home from my then current girlfriend's residence which was in Higher Bebbington. Would you believe the signal lamp was still burning just as brightly!

This is probably a good point at which to relate a favourite anecdote of my good friend the late Norman Jones about Herbert at work in Mouldsworth signal box. Entitled 'Herbert Loses a Train' it is taken from a sound recording made by Norman *circa* 1959. Essentially it goes that Herbert has passed a freight from Dee Marsh through to his mate Sam in Delamere box, when he 'bells' it through there is an unseemingly long pause before Herbert loses patience and calls Sam up to enquire if he has received it, Sam replies that he hasn't got it! Herbert says, 'But I give 'im to you!' Again one hears Sam's squeaky reply on the phone affirming the negative, Herbert turns to Norman and says, 'A've lost a train!'

Guess where we went for our holiday in 1957? Right first time, Margate again! This time my dad decided that he couldn't handle another stint on the 'Great way round' so we took the more direct route via Euston. This time (for a change) a pristine 'Baby Scot' was our steed and the journey to the capital was made without issue. Well, that is if one ignores the continuous barrage of questions that my poor dad had to put up with from yours truly. Key questions requiring immediate and precise answers would start as soon as we left the station, the first being, 'Where does that line go to dad?' - 'Warrington and Manchester' came the reply, this was soon followed by another such question - the reply this time being 'Whitchurch' and so on all the way to Euston! It was this sort of activity that earned me the sobriquet '*intelligentsia pestilentsia*'. Another precious recollection of the journey is that of having a proper 'silver service' lunch in a 12-wheel ex-LMS dining car. Who today can recall the 'clickety click, click' of riding in such a superb vehicle at speed? Perhaps the most enduring memory of the journey was that of standing on the platform on the 'Chatham' side of Victoria station looking at our rather grubby Urie 'King Arthur' and listening to my dad make clearly audible and disparaging remarks about the girth of the chimney and how it would make a nice 'jerry' for Bessie Braddock! You can't take an LMS man anywhere can you?

Trips out on that particular holiday numbered runs to Dover and Folkestone on different days. I distinctly remember walking along the Dover promenade between the Marine station and what is today the Eastern Dock, and what should come trundling along the street but a little Wainwright 'P' class 0-6-0T hauling a brake van. No trace of that street dock line exists today. The highlight of the trip out to Folkestone a few days later was witnessing an evenly distributed quartet of 'R1' class 0-6-0 tanks straining away at a boat train on the steeply-graded harbour branch. If only I could go back with my modern video camera and capture the sight and sounds of that little lot! The following year the old South Eastern & Chatham Railway engines were replaced with ex-GWR panniers of the '57XX' class which made much lighter but less entertaining work of the job. The only event that has stuck steadfastly in my mind

Work in progress re-roofing Bangor engine shed in August 1957.   *J.M. Dunn*

concerning the return journey was my father's utter infuriation on arrival at Euston to be told that, because we were travelling on a railway pass, we were not allowed to board the 'Midday Scot'. Apparently the powers that be had decreed that second class pass holders were not allowed to travel on that particular train on Saturdays! You can imagine his display of verbal pyrotechnics on being told that by the lowly and unsuspecting ticket collector at the barrier! We journeyed home on a heavy relief train behind a hard working Stanier class '5' all the way to Crewe.

This particular year (1957) saw the start of what was to become, for a few years at least, a regular event as my dad joined me at my grandmother's for a week of gadding about around North Wales during the autumn half-term holiday. We did the usual walks such as up Conway Mountain etc., but other more profound' activities were indulged in! The first of these special activities was a trip to Bangor, nothing special in that? Well there was as it was a trip to see my dad's friend Max Dunn at Bangor shed. Max had been the shedmaster there since 1944 after a wartime spell in Coventry and was now nearing the end of what was to be his penultimate year of his long railway career. At the time of visiting, the shed was in the throes of receiving its new roof and I distinctly remember Max meeting us off the train with the purpose of guiding us safely through the morass of building work that was in progress. Looking back on it I don't recall any of the shed staff wearing such a contrivance as a hard hat as pieces of old roofing and bricks etc. made regular journeys earthwards! (*Further reference to this visit is made in the next chapter.*)

The year 1958 brought what was probably the most memorable holiday of my entire childhood. The destination was Rothesay on the Isle of Bute in the Firth of Clyde. The choice I think was inspired by my Dad's desire to revisit an area where he had spent a number of past holidays in his misspent youth chasing the lassies on the Isles of Bute and Arran!

The greatest thrill for me, probably of the entire holiday, was standing on Crewe station watching 'The Caledonian' come in with the smart headboard adorning our steed which was a green 'Duchess'. We fairly took off along the level stretches north of Crewe and my dad with his watch looking out for mileposts logged an honest 100 mph before we got to Warrington. Scratching his head, he got up from his seat and went out into the corridor. After a few minutes he returned, grinning, with the words, 'No wonder we're going so damn fast, she's only got seven on!' 'The Caledonian' was a modern lightweight BR express introduced in the early 1950s to augment the Scottish services. It is something we take for granted today with our 4,000 bhp electrics, but 40 years or so ago there were few trains on which one could travel at those sort of speeds. The journey continued with great rapidity and we fairly romped up Shap. However, on reaching Carlisle the engine was changed for a Polmadie 'Britannia' and progress after that seemed snail-like in comparison with the 'Lizzie's' performance. Oh yes, whilst we were standing in Citadel station I got my first glimpse of an LNER engine, a polished 'A3' entering from the North on a train off the Waverley Route. The journey continued in the more sedate style and on entering the approaches over the Clyde into Glasgow Central I distinctly recall seeing the bright orange and green trams in the streets below.

A slow and grimy Fairburn tank-hauled suburban train took us out to Gourock, where a 30 minute wait on the pier revealed an interesting selection of Clyde shipping plying to and fro, amongst which was a smart little steamer of the black and red-funnelled David MacBrayne fleet. Our conveyance duly presented itself in the form of an ultra modern diesel-powered vehicle ferry. Not exactly 'roll on-roll off', the cars and vans waiting beside us on the pier had to be hoisted aboard by a ship-mounted derrick! But progress in those days had advanced to the point where road vehicle movements between the Isles had warranted the construction of vessels with a special low level open foredeck designed specifically for the transportation of road vehicles. Anyway I digress, by now the rain was coming down in that fine drizzle so typical of the Celtic regions and I shall never forget that group of students in the ship's bar singing away with great gusto as our small vessel pitched and rolled its way across to Dunoon ... 'Tom Brown's body lies a-rotting in the grave ... etc., etc.'

Almost all of that delightful sabbatical was spent aboard small ships visiting the various places of interest in the Firth of Clyde, Arran of course was early on the list, Brodick being our destination. The ladies (my mother and her mother - 'Nainy') were dispatched to look at the nearby castle whilst *mon père* and I sought out a certain bungalow. The knock on the door was answered by a charming lady in her mid-fifties ... 'Jack', she exclaimed ... I forget what happened next (honest) but what's it got to do with railways anyway! Other places of interest visited included Campbeltown and Machrihanish Bay on the Mull of Kintyre where my mum got a great thrill from dipping her toes in the Atlantic Ocean for the first time in her life! (All signs of the 2 ft 3 in. gauge line had by then been obliterated by the drifting dunes.)

We visited on one long trip the neighbouring Loch Lomond by taking a steamer to Arrochar at the far northern end of Loch Long, followed by a short bus journey to Tarbet which is about two-thirds of the way up Loch Lomond. From here we boarded the pretty all-white steamer that plied the Loch, this took us down to Balloch pier where I was to have my second 'North Eastern' experience. Awaiting us was a suburban train of about six coaches hauled by a 'J39' class engine, this took us tender-first to Dumbarton. Here it ran around the train to take us in the reverse direction along the northern bank of the Clyde to Craigendoran Pier.

Here most of the train's occupants alighted with us to await our steamer back to Rothesay. The highlight of the day came around the point in the form of that beautiful little railway paddle steamer *Waverley* resplendent in its black hull with white upper works topped off with its twin cream funnels. I shall always remember my dad and I going down to the engine room there to witness its twin green horizontal cylinders and massive cranks rotating under the thrust of its huge green connecting rods. Some days later the journey back home to Chester was made via Wemyss Bay and a very crowded train, again 'Brit'-hauled from Glasgow this time all the way to Crewe.

Blue Squares and Yellow Diamonds

The autumn half-term week this year included two 'special' trips or visits. The first was a short one distance wise as it constituted a walk across to the Junction shed! By now some 13 years had elapsed since my dad worked at the shed as a fitter and yet some of his contemporaries were still working there in the same jobs. One of these men kindly showed yours truly around the various points of interest whilst my dad chatted to his old mates. By now the shed had received its new roof and so was in a far more presentable condition than Bangor had been a year earlier. Fixed in my memory are scenes of the machine/fitting shop with its large green-painted lathe and radial arm drill. I think I was too young to fully appreciate the significance of the wheel drop but I do remember being agog at the sight of a class '5' slipping like fury as it laboured with a train of coal wagons, dragging them right through the shed and out onto the long rear siding, the wheels emitting a stream of sparks as the engine fought to get to grips with the rails. Disappointingly for me most of the visit was spent over in the carriage shed listening to the foreman fitter extolling the virtues of the new diesels which by now included several other types beyond the original 'Derby Lightweights' which had 'yellow diamonds' and so could not be hooked up to the 'blue squares', etc., etc. Even at that age I preferred the dirty old steam engines and couldn't conjure up much enthusiasm for these new intruders. The most poignant point of the visit came when dad asked where his old friend and (leading fitter) colleague Tom Maclay was: 'in hospital' came the subdued reply that didn't augur well. Having gained details of the ward we made off to Llandudno hospital later that afternoon. We almost bumped into Tom coming out of a bathroom when we arrived on the men's surgical ward. My dad was stunned, here was a man that 13 years earlier had sacrificed his own chances of promotion for my dad's advancement, sallow, shrunken and obviously seriously ill. As I recall Tom had been suffering with prostate problems and I don't think he survived very long after his operation.

Earlier in this hallowed dissertation I made mention of a trip up to Blaenau Ffestiniog. Well it was another profoundly interesting day out during that same week in late October 1958. We boarded the front seats of the 10.35 am from Llandudno two-coach Derby Lightweight dmu at the Junction which was timed to arrive at Blaenau Ffestiniog at 12.09 pm. To this day, not withstanding my original lack of enthusiasm, I can recall the enchantment of this new mode of rail travel, watching the driver working the throttle and brakes with their characteristic hiss of air as they were applied and released, not to mention looking at the speedo and rev. counter which were things previously unknown to me. I think my dad found the whole process somewhat amusing too as I later heard him relate that driving a diesel was little more than twiddling your thumbs! Anyway the journey although in typical gloomy and damp weather was enchanting especially as we wound our way beyond Bettws-y-Coed up the Lledr valley. The pin prick of light visible just after we entered that 2 miles 206 yds-long Ffestiniog tunnel that gradually got larger as we neared the exit is an especially enduring memory and its an experience that has been enjoyed in more recent years from the front passenger seats, at least whilst the old 'Heritage' Metro-Cammell dmus remained in use.* We emerged into

---

* Since writing they have been displaced by class '150' and '153' respectively double and single carriage units.

that not so rare speciality of Blaenau Ffestiniog, incessant rain and low cloud clinging to those depressing slate strewn mountains. Not to worry, I had my trusty school gabardine mack to protect me. We left the warm dry confines of our dmu and set forth to explore the 'Slate Capital of the World'. First thing to catch young 'Robbo's' eye was of course the myriads of rusting narrow gauge slate trucks across in the goods yard. Remember this was that long folorn period between closure and re-opening of the 2 ft gauge Festiniog Railway (notice the spelling, one 'f'). Further down the road I espied a Great Western pannier tank shunting in the yard at Central station. Now this was a real surprise as I didn't realize at that point in time that there was a GWR line in that cheery town. Well in that grey drizzling weather we soon got fed up of trailing around and so retraced our steps to the North station to return on the 12.27 pm return working of our earlier conveyance. The guard seeing our soaked countenances, and knowing my dad, very kindly placed our mackintoshs on a hook in his cubby hole that had a hot air supply running through it, so by the time we got back to the Junction all were thoroughly dry.

The year 1959 was a far less of an adventure, the destination being born out of indecision: we almost went to Bournemouth, what a shame, a trip on the Somerset & Dorset sadly missed, but we wound up going to Southport! Whilst the holiday was nothing to write home about we did take a day trip to Windermere, this via the now defunct line between Crossens and Preston. The Windermere branch with its dark and claustraphobic terminus (the trainshed is now a supermarket) in those days was teeming with Fowler 2-6-4 tanks, or so it seemed to me anyway. Highlight of the holiday for me was a visit one morning to Southport shed, where my dad met up with the shedmaster whose name I can't recall save that he was quite elderly and must have been nearing his retirement. He was a crony of my dad's from days spent at that earlier mentioned L&Y shed, Sowerby Bridge. Anyway, he was a nice bloke who welcomed us and proudly showed off his empire. That was where I first saw, in close up, the Aspinall 2-4-2Ts that my dad had admired some 10 years previously. The return journey home was memorable for one thing, the ticket collector at Liverpool Exchange station asked me where I lived. 'Chester', said I, 'No you don't' came the reply, 'You come from the Welsh side of the border near Chester, I can tell by your accent!' I must say that I felt somewhat crestfallen as I always believed that I spoke with an English accent. Still it goes to show how an astute ticket collector, who was an obvious student of local dialects, had acquired the ability to differentiate twixt small changes in dialect, something that I must confess to admiring and even trying to emulate to this day!

There was another event that took place a month or two earlier in 1959, which I think deserves a mention, and that was my first-ever school trip. You will recall from previous chapters that I attended Broughton County Primary school and it was the tradition of the said institution that every summer the members of the two senior forms (i.e. 10 and 11 year olds) were taken on a day's outing to some place or places of interest. As on previous excursions the day began with an early rendezvous and head count in the school yard and then we were marched in crocodile fashion to Broughton & Bretton station, there to assemble in an 'orderly' fashion on the up platform. I distinctly recall my dad arriving some seconds before his train pulled in behind one of his Fowler '4Fs' (his

BR Standard 2-6-4T No. 80006 leaves Broughton & Bretton station with a Chester-Denbigh train on 7th May, 1959. *H.F. Wheeller Collection*

timing was always precise!) and then some 10 minutes after the departure of his train to Saltney Ferry and Chester our train of six open corridor thirds of period II vintage arrived behind what was to be our steed for the day, a Fowler 2-6-4T of Chester shed. The train had already picked up kids from Mold and Pen-y-Fford schools and so was at least half-full, but the carriages had been clearly marked with the names of each school on the windows. So having boarded in our 'orderly fashion' our steed trundled us off, bunker first to Chester. Here the kids of Saltney & Saltney Ferry Junior schools were waiting, I think Saltney Ferry station had been discounted as too small to hold the numbers involved. The bi-directional platform 14 was used and our Fowler ran around the train so facing the direction of travel - Llandudno!

The sun was shining as we left Chester and did so all day, it was a scorcher typical of that long hot summer of 1959. On arrival at Llandudno we again were assembled on the main arrival platform 3 which with its carriage drive was an excellent marshalling area for a trainload of errant juniors. Our crocodiles then proceeded down Vaughn Road and across Mostyn Street and onto the promenade. From here we marched along the seafront and onto the pier and so to the end of it where our next conveyance was waiting, the steamship *St Seiriol* of the Liverpool and North Wales Steam Packet Co. We ate our sandwiches (prepared by our devoted mothers) aboard the ship before enjoying that singularly superb sea journey across Conway Bay and around Puffin Island and into the Menai Straits. (One of the great losses to the area's tourist attractions was the demise of the steamer services to Menai Bridge, the Isle of Man and Liverpool that this steamship company provided. On a fine day the view of Snowdonia from a ship crossing Conway Bay was unbeatable.) On arrival at

Menai Bridge pier Crosville Motor Services had very 'kindly' laid on a fleet of the most modern cream-liveried 'Forward Control' Bristol single-deckers to take us back down the road to Beaumaris. Here we were let loose like a pack of caged hooligans around the castle and its myriad dark passageways. On a humorous note I recall buying my parents small gifts in one of the village shops: my mum got a dressmaking tape measure whilst my dad got a wooden letter rack with the words 'All the world's queer except thee and me and even thee's a little queer!' (We must remember that the word queer had no other connotation than strange in those days.) Anyway needless to say it tickled him pink and it was years later before I saw the joke!

Our small fleet of buses eventually deposited a very weary and footsore crowd of kids and their equally weary teachers at the bus station in Bangor from where the various school groups went off in search of supper. As I recall, we settled on eating fish and chips at a café not far from the station. I think it was about 6.30 pm and the time had come to make the journey home so we all repaired to the station. There standing at platform 1 was that most welcome sight of our trusty Fowler with the same train that had deposited us at Llandudno some hours earlier. How well organized BR was in those days and so accommodating! Read on, the story is not yet over!

As the song goes, we travelled home from Bangor on that eastbound train … well er, not quite! You see the Saltney crowd had alighted at Chester all according to plan, the train had reversed and this time manned by men of Rhyl shed was merrily making its way back up the Mold branch, we passed Mold Junction at a healthy pace and our coach resounded to the strains of 'Knick-knack paddy wack give a dog a bone … this old train went rolling through!' The latter words were my addition for we went belting through Broughton & Bretton station at about 40 mph and accelerating! We glimpsed our parents grouped around the crossing gates looking on in astonishment, my dad, needless to say, was in the signal box chatting to an even more astonished signalman (Dennis Jones). The road was always set at clear for down passenger workings due to the fact that the gates were right off the platform edge and the locomotive would always stop on the crossing. The singing subsided into a deathly silence as the train's Broughton-bound inhabitants realized they might not be getting home as planned! For my part it was great, here we were getting more ride for our money; anyway my dad would sort it out, he always did! By now the train was tearing down the short bank which was always used by down freights as a run up for the 1 in 43 of Kinnerton bank. We went through Kinnerton station at what must have been an all time speed record as there was no stop booked there. Whether the 'flight crew' realized their gaff as the sun began to stream in through the westward turning bunker spectacles is not and probably never will be known but when Pen-y-fford was reached (in record time) they were left in no doubt as the Broughton signalman had the wires buzzing! (No doubt augmented by a crowd of hysterical parents in his box.) With much verbiage and scratching of heads the driver went off across the line to speak to Control from the box, meanwhile the Hope and Pen-y-Fford kids alighted a few minutes earlier than expected.

After the driver got back on the footplate rumours of a 'diesel' started to circulate, these didn't make much sense but we still had the Mold kids on the train so off we went. As we pulled into Mold station the rumour took shape, there in the up platform stood a brand new two-car Gloucester Railway Carriage & Wagon Co. unit replete with its 'cat's whiskers' on the front. We were ordered off the train and over the bridge to board what to us in those days was a fantastic contrivance and so much better than the grimy old thing we had been on for most of the day. Well the contrivance got us back to Broughton in what seemed to be next to no time at all; my pal David and I 'bagged' the back seat so that we could view the receding journey (teachers got the front seats!). Not many people can claim to have ridden in a dmu on the Chester, Mold & Denbigh line save for those who indulged themselves in railtours towards the end of the line's existence. Right up until the cessation of the line's passenger services at the end of April 1962 suburban coaches were steam-hauled. To finish off we all got off our beloved dmu at Broughton to be greeted by some very relieved parents. My dad later laconically explained that due to an oversight at Control the driver's notice didn't have a stop at Broughton & Bretton marked on it. It was sheer good fortune that the diesel had been at Mold on a driver training trip as there was no way the crew of the Fowler were going to backtrack for us as they were booked through to Rhyl and had to get there before the line was closed for the night!

There was one final event that sticks forever in my memory from that long hot summer of 1959. Our next door neighbours had swopped their home with that of some family relatives who lived near Blackpool. The arrangement was to last a fortnight and effectively was the basis of a 'cheapo' summer holiday for both families! Our 'new neighbours' gained ready access to North Wales and the Chester area for their troubles. Now these people were very friendly and offered to take me with them in their smart MK I Ford 'Consul' on a day trip to Bala. It wasn't often one got the chance of a ride in a six-seater with a column shift in those days! On arrival at our chosen destination it was decided that a spot below the main road bordering the northern shore of the lake would be used for a picnic. You can imagine my delight when very soon along the opposite shore and at a prodigious speed came an ex-GWR '43XX' Mogul with a six-coach train heading eastwards. Not so very long afterwards came a similar entourage, this time running in the opposite direction towards Dolgelly (nowadays spelt Dolgellau). We spent about two hours at that charming spot and in that time I must have espied at least a half dozen more trains all hauled by gleaming 'Manors' and Moguls. Remember it was a Saturday in the high summer, and what was normally a country branch line was then handling an inordinately high volume of traffic. Picture if you will an entire train at speed hauled by a gleaming green Mogul with its polished brass adornments reflected in the still waters of the lake … magic, pure magic! The following year I was able to sample that stretch of line at first hand … however, more about that later.

One other small but not insignificant event occurred in August of that year. My sister Ann and her husband Ron had come home for the first time since emigrating to Canada two years earlier. After a three week holiday they returned by rail from Chester to Gatwick via Euston and on a typically hot Saturday afternoon my dad and I saw them off from Chester General. Just before their train came in, the future arrived! It was my first ever sighting of a type '4' English

Electric diesel as she rolled in gracefully with a Holyhead-bound train off the Crewe line. Rumour had it amongst the local railway fraternity, that when it was first mooted that these new locomotives were to be diagrammed for Euston-Crewe-Holyhead workings they would not get beyond Chester. It was thought they would 'split' the curved diamond crossings on the west side of the station! This of course, was on account of their exceedingly long bogie wheelbase. Unfortunately for us steam addicts they didn't ... the rest is history.

The annual 1960 summer school trip was further afield than the previous year, but in time honoured fashion it began in the same way from the up platform at Broughton & Bretton station. This time the train rolled in behind a BR class '4' '75XXX' and the destination was the ancient city of York. The first thing of note to happen was a yelp of delight from one of my chums as we approached Mold Junction shed yard, 'Cor look at that Wessie!' he exclaimed. There standing on the turntable was a gleaming 'Hall' class locomotive that seemed to put all the other engines in the yard to shame. In April of that year the ex-GWR shed at Chester West had closed in preparation for dieselization and from that date all Western Region engines terminating their freight diagrams in the nearby Saltney yard went forward to Mold Junction for servicing and turnarounds.

Chester West shed *circa* 1955 seen on a dull day. Careful inspection reveals a number of men grouped around the side of '51XX' class 2-6-2T No. 5160 looking at the crosshead area. GWR sheds rarely installed wheel drops and the lifting gantry to the left of the building has recently been employed to lift an engine over a pair of driving wheels. The wheels further away appear to belong to a tender. As a youngster I remember being intrigued by the old steam crane that resided alongside the shed, its tall chimney can just be seen. As I recall the shed was a cramped 'mucky hole' that didn't do justice to the cleanliness of its engines or its seeming importance as a highly visible (from London Midland and Western Region trains) main line shed!   *J.M. Dunn*

After picking up the Saltney school party at Chester we departed down the
Warrington line and a rare sighting was glimpsed as we ran beneath the West
Cheshire branch as we approached Helsby. Hauling an ex-Shell tanker train up
the bank towards Mouldsworth was another former GWR engine off its regular
patch, this time a grimy '28XX' 2-8-0. (It probably worked as far as Northwich
before returning to Chester via Mickle Trafford.) Our journey took us onward
to Warrington where, before joining the West Coast main line at Moore, I espied
the stirring sight of a 'Lizzie' (Stanier 'Princess') passing us at speed with a long
train up on the main line heading north. We diverged sharply to the right at
Warrington through Arpley and along the now defunct line via Latchford and
Lymm. Our journey was a mass of interest for me as we went via Stockport and
Guide Bridge where of course I spied the Woodhead line electrics. Apart from
a fleeting glimpse of the ancient overhead-supplied Lancaster/Morecambe/
Heysham electrics a couple of years earlier, I had never seen the likes before in
the flesh, except in my dad's *Railway Gazette* which was full of the line's
progress some years earlier. Our excursion went on up through the Standedge
tunnel, which at 5,324 yds is the second longest in the country, and out into
West Yorkshire through Huddersfield and Wakefield and on to York. Most of
the day was spent doing the 'boring' things like Clifford's Tower, the Shambles,
Museum and the obligatory cruise on the Ouse, etc. Prior to returning to the
station we got to see the one thing that held my attention ... the railway
museum! Not the splendid affair in Leeman Road that exists today but a
somewhat more modest one that hid directly beside the station in an old and
dark ex-goods station building. Very much a celebration of things Great
Northern and North Eastern railways, it held such treasures as the Ivatt Atlantic
Henry Oakley and that strange single-wheeler tank engine *Aerolite* amongst
others. With little time left for trainspotting on the main line platforms, I did see
a couple of 'B1s' and the '5X' 'Jubilee' No. 45698 *Mars* that got the road south-
west to Wakefield just before us. The journey home seemed endless but this
time we were deposited safely back at Broughton, unlike the previous year!

The 1960 summer holiday for some reason, probably financial, failed to
present an exciting new destination so what was a time honoured practice of
taking a fortnight at the Junction came into play. This meant a holiday at my
grandmother's as she was always known in the family at her home at 5 Marl
Drive, which was almost opposite the station. Now strange as it may seem after
such exotica as Margate and the Isle of Bute the jolly old Junction still had its
attractions. Naturally having lived there for five years I still had acquaintances
and I knew my way around all those intimate little nooks like the old
brickworks which was adjacent to the sheds. Although never a trainspotter in
the accepted sense of the word I was always in my element when within sight
and sound of a busy railway line. So my aunt's pet corgi got lots of walks in
such places that were entirely boring to a member of the canine clan! Back in
those halcyon days the Junction was still a very important place from a railway
point of view and one of our old neighbours from St David's Avenue, a certain
Mr Perkins, was employed at the station as the publicity officer for the area. At
the time he was plugging something very important, indeed if he was to be
believed he had a lot to do with its initial inception some years earlier! He

The 'North Wales Land Cruise' is hauled by Ivatt class '2' 2-6-0 No. 464245 as it heads south through Barmouth station *circa* 1952. The stock of this train was a pre-war mixture and the last coach, a brake composite, had extended valances betraying its origin as part of the old 'Coronation Scot' consist. The anti-clockwise working was later to become known as the 'Welsh Chieftain'. *J.M. Dunn*

Ex-GWR 2-6-0 No. 7314 of Brecon shed in the bay platform at Barmouth *circa* 1962. The engine was working a Ruabon-Barmouth-Chester turn. *Norman Jones*

caught us on his way home from the station one evening and knowing my father well began extolling the virtues of 'his' baby. The item in question was that legendary train the 'North Wales Land Cruise'. My mother who still suffered from her leg wound and liked any sort of trip that enabled interesting sightseeing *sans* promenading was well and truly sold by our man's pitch and ordered my dad to use his 'PT' card to buy tickets the very next day.

When today I look at all those miles of overgrown trackbed that the train traversed it brings a twinge of remorse tinged with sheer thankfulness that we took the trip. For a number of years previously the special ex-'Coronation Scot' carriages used in the train's formation had been stored on the Cob siding during the winter months and it had become something of a curiosity to me to sample their interiors. That opportunity came a day or two later at about 9 am on platform 1 when the train entered the station from its starting place of Llandudno behind a BR class '4' '75XXX' of the Junction shed. Our seats were reserved in an open coach opulently finished in oak panelling: it was a bit like a royal saloon with armchairs positioned around tables, music played over loudspeakers at either end of the saloon. As the train pulled out our 'host' welcomed us aboard and announced that a full running commentary on the route would be given over the Tannoy system after the train left its last pick-up point which was Rhyl. More lucky people entrained at Colwyn Bay and then it was non-stop to Rhyl where the engine uncoupled and went on shed to turn. It then coupled to the other end of the train and took us to Foryd Junction where we turned due south down the Vale of Clwyd line. I distinctly remember catching my first ever sight of Rhuddlan Castle from the train window and listening to our man on the microphone giving a potted history of the edifice. I have memories of seeing the River Clwyd, by then a mere stream, alongside the line up in the Eyarth Gorge, crossing the Dee Bridge on the outskirts of the metropolis of Corwen in that bucolic setting in the upper reaches of the Dee Valley. One can at least look forward to the day when the Llangollen Railway finally pushes its rails back into that one time pretty (and important) railway outpost!

Memories persist of most of the occupants of our carriage leaning over to the right-hand window to get a glimpse of Bala Lake as we ran beside it, again to the accompaniment of our host telling us about the legend of the lost town beneath the lake. Apart from stopping at places like Dolgelly to allow up trains to pass, inevitably hauled by a '63XX' Mogul, we didn't have a scheduled stop until we reached Aberdovey, and that after reversing at Barmouth Junction (then recently renamed Morfa Mawddach). It is interesting to note that, by this time, it was not possible to run from the Dolgelly line and south onto the Cambrian coast line via the connecting curve as it had been truncated into a siding at either end and its *raison d'etre* was to serve as a reversing triangle for engines that had worked trains from Ruabon to neighbouring Barmouth, prior to them working back up the Dolgelly-Ruabon line.

Having run around the train the engine then proceeded tender first with the train down the Aberdovey where we stopped for lunch and a break of two hours to explore the delights of the harbour. In those days the harbour branch was still extant and terminated on the all-timber jetty with short off-shoots

Ex-Midland Railway '3F' class 0-6-0 No. 43618 of Rhyl shed gets away from Corwen on the ex-LNWR branch to Ruthin in May 1961 with the Saturdays-excepted class 'K' pick-up goods departing Corwen at 12.20 pm. It is seen crossing the lattice girder bridge over the River Dee in a bucolic setting.

Norman Jones

Norman Jones has turned his camera around to catch the same train 100 yards further along the line towards Gwyddelwern. Guard Arthur Davies stands on the rear balcony of his brake van. By this time apart from seasonal 'Cambrian Radio Cruise' special workings this was the only train of the day, out and back from Rhyl. The train formation would be made up in Denbigh, and what we see is typical with just a few coal empties being returned to Denbigh.

Norman Jones

running from wagon turntables. The return journey was memorable for sights of Harlech Castle, '45XX' small Prairies at Portmadoc and my first ever view of the Festiniog Railway and that marvellous, but now long gone, three-doll bracket signal silhouetted in the evening light on the Cob outside the harbour station. The return journey was via Afonwen and Caernarvon: I think we wound up back at the Junction at about 7.30 pm, tired but very satisfied after an excellent and memorable day out.

Early in 1961 rumours abounded at Mold Junction that passenger working on the Mold and Denbigh line was going to cease. Not surprising when one noted the appalling lack of patronage during the day: sometimes a class '4' locomotive would be in charge of three coaches carrying no more than three or four passengers! It was soon to be a reality to be confronted by all those regular users of the line, one of whom was my father. Public notice was served sometime later that cessation of all passenger services would take place the following year. My dad resolved to keep his own means of transport to and from the shed, albeit in an improved form over his push bike. A Phillips 'Panda Plus' moped was duly purchased from Halfords in Chester (I think the price was somewhere in the region of £40) and in May of that year I accompanied him by train one Saturday morning to Mold where a provisional licence was obtained from the local vehicle licencing office. After a cursory wander around the town we returned to the station for our train to Broughton. A Stanier 2-6-4T of Chester shed duly arrived with the three-coach working from Denbigh, the driver caught my dad's eye and called us up to the footplate. Yours truly ascended and was promptly offered the fireman's seat. It was an easy run, mostly downhill, with stops at Llong, Pen-y-Ffordd, and Kinnerton (Padeswood and Hope Exchange having closed a few years earlier). I just wish we had had the footplate trip on the outward working, the ascent of Kinnerton bank would have been much more entertaining. Well that was my penultimate trip on the branch beyond Broughton because closure was announced for 30th April, 1962.

That year's holiday was something of a watershed as it was the last year that we all ventured forth on a typical family holiday together. By now, my mother, who suffered continual and debilitating leg pain, had decided that if my father and I were to enjoy our common interest of walking and exploring at the expense of leaving her and her mother behind while we did the 'exploring', then she would rather we went off on a holiday of our own. A somewhat magnanimous gesture and not untypical of my good-hearted mum! The choice for this year was to be the pleasant seaside town of Bray in County Wicklow, Ireland. The journey to Holyhead was by a train that ran daily from Crewe and was known by railwaymen as the 'Newspapers'. The new English Electric type '4' diesel-electrics (later to become known as 'Whistlers' due to their unmistakable whistling growl) had ousted the Stanier Pacifics from all but a few West Coast main line turns and the 'Newspapers' had become a daily roster for one of the Crewe 'Duchesses'. The train left Chester at about 11.30 am and was invariably heavily loaded, hence the choice of motive power. As arranged my grandmother was waiting to board the train when we arrived at the Junction and Holyhead was reached without issue in nice time to catch the afternoon sailing to Dun Laoghaire. In those days one only had to cross the open

The north end of Crewe station in the early 1960s. 'Royal Scot' class 4-6-0 No. 46155 *The Lancer* unhooks and draws forward from a Manchester- or Liverpool-bound working. The 'AL1' class Bo-Bo electric locomotive on the left will couple up to complete the journey to the, by then, electrified final destination. This was the practice until the lines south of Crewe were themselves electrified.

George Carr

Crewe North shed in the early 1960s. This view shows two Stanier 'Duchess' Pacifics. No. 46244 *King George VI* on the left displays the open running plate style front end of a former streamlined engine. On the right No. 46250 *City of Lichfield* displays the curved and original style front end.

George Carr

concourse from platform 1 to board the ship, which in this event was the *Hibernia*. A relatively modern (BR) vessel that, together with sister ship *Cambria*, plied the busy ferry route twixt Holyhead and Dun Laoghaire.

In our usual fashion my dad and I parked the ladies in the (first class) saloon and went off to 'explore' the ship. Somewhere up on the boat deck near the bridge my dad found himself in conversation with a uniformed officer. I don't recall the gist of the conversation but it was little more than an exchange of pleasantries. Well, departure time arrived and we stayed and witnessed the departure from the harbour and once out to sea retreated to join the ladies in the warmth of the saloon. We hadn't been there long when a sailor approached my dad with the words, 'Excuse me sir, the Captain would like to know if you and your son would like to come up to the bridge?' I didn't need asking twice! If you haven't guessed it, the man my dad had been talking to earlier was none other than the skipper himself and he was there to welcome us into his hallowed domain. Having shown us around the bridge and its various fascinating paraphernalia the *coup de grâce* for me was the radar booth. In those days it resembled a 'Woolies' photo booth with a thick curtain over the entrance to keep out unwanted light, very much a green cathode ray screen with its characteristic sweeping beam. Perhaps antiquated by modern standards, it held enormous fascination for me. Why, I could see just about every ship in the Irish Sea south of the Calf of Man right down St George's Channel beyond St David's Head, and in some detail too! After a calm crossing we arrived at the station pier at Dun Laoghaire which, as many contemporary travellers will remember, had a fierce right-hand curve on its two platform roads. On the outer curve the platform gap at the mid-point of each coach had to be seen to be believed and bridging boards were being used to ease entry into the carriage doorways. By 1961 the Metro-Vick 550 hp Bo-Bo diesels reigned supreme on all but the least important workings. I recall seeing only one steam locomotive for the whole two weeks of our sabbatical. It was an 0-6-0 goods engine of dubious parentage (probably an old 'J8' of the Dublin & South Eastern Railway) shunting at the main line station of the said arrival port. The diesel locomotives were everywhere and with their poorly-maintained 2-stroke Crossley engines emitted so much smoke that they resembled a steam engine with casing on when going at full bore! One journey worthy of note during the holiday was a day excursion to Killarney and back from Amiens Street, Dublin. My dad rightfully commented on the superior ride afforded by the Irish 5 ft 3 in. broad gauge, more space in the carriages too!

As remarked earlier, passenger services on the Chester, Mold, Denbigh & Ruthin line were to cease as from 30th April, 1962. My dad and I resolved to travel to Denbigh and back before the fateful day arrived. In the event we cut it a bit fine and didn't actually make the journey until the final Saturday. We boarded the 1.29 pm from Broughton & Bretton which had left Chester at 1.18 pm. Motive power was a BR Standard class '4' 75XXX', by then the most prolific hauler on the line. There was no outward show that this was to be the last day of services and when we arrived at Kinnerton I recall a rather portly 'farm' lady plus little girl and large canine accomplice entering our compartment. The large 'farm' lady sat opposite myself in a window seat and thankfully didn't mind me

BR Standard class '4' 4-6-0 No. 75033 of Mold Junction shed approaches Mold with the 5.00 pm from Denbigh on 28th April, 1962 - last day of service. *M. Mensing*

BR Standard class '4' 4-6-0 No. 75010 of Llandudno Junction shed arrives at Llong station with the 6.35 pm Chester-Ruthin train on 28th April, 1962. Note the typical Francis Thompson country station building which includes the station master's house. This building still survives along with its siblings at Broughton & Bretton and Hope & Pen-y-Ffordd. The characteristically low platforms required wooden steps for the less agile passengers, a set of steps can just be seen on the left. *M. Mensing*

having the droplight pulled down someway ... I say thankfully because she emitted something of an extraordinarily strong aroma! She sat there blissfully unaware of the effect her 'ring of confidence' was having on the rest of the passengers for her entire journey which lasted until the train reached Star Crossing Halt, whereupon she stepped down from the carriage to be greeted by the station master/porter in a somewhat familiar manner indicating that she was a regular traveller! Somehow I've always felt that she was probably so blissfully ignorant of her surroundings that she turned up at the station the following week to get a return train!

The next little episode concerning the farming community was to occur just after entering the single line section beyond Bodfari. The train started to slow to a walking pace, I leaned out of the window to observe a number of sheep on the line that seemed intent on running ahead of the train. The driver opened the cylinder taps and they fairly leapt over the lineside fencing back whence they came and we were off again! On arrival at Denbigh we left the train, which continued on to Ruthin, and we walked up into the town and on up to the castle. Not much to say about that final return journey other than it departed Denbigh at 5.00 pm and again was hauled by a BR class '4', this time 6B's No. 75033 did the honours. I think the final train left Chester to some fanfare later at 8.30 pm behind a 2-6-4T, which the local rag reported as being a 4-6-4T to my utter consternation!

Fairburn 2-6-4T No. 42209 of Chester shed pauses at Hope & Pen-y-Ffordd station with the last ever up working, the 7.30 pm from Ruthin, on 28th April, 1962. There was no fuss or fanfare to mark the occasion.   *M. Mensing*

The summer of 1962 did not produce an exciting destination so it was back to the Junction once again for the last two weeks in August. Some weeks earlier my trusty friend David Willoughby had requested that I accompanied him for a week's stay at relatives in Ulster. As there were to be no parents present for the journey my mother declined the invitation on my behalf but countered, after checking with my grandmother, with an alternative offer of a visit to the Junction. By now we were 13 years old and it was deemed safe for us to make train journeys of short duration on our own providing the destination was somewhere well known.

We had a great week, earning our keep by exercising the dog on a regular basis. I aquainted my friend with my knowledge of the area around the shed and brickworks (which had by now closed down) and it was during one of these trips that I first encountered the word 'Semi'. We had arrived at the parapet of the bridge over the main line just east of the station where, not unusually, were grouped a number of trainspotters, one of which turned to me in a state of excitment and asked if I had seen the 'Semi' go through. I have to confess that I had a few minutes earlier seen the 'Semi' but did not know what he was talking about. My mate put me wise, 'I think he means the "Duchess"' said he. The aforementioned 'Newspapers' had just trundled into the station behind a Stanier Pacific. Do you know it was over 35 years later that I discovered the origin of that strange name! 'Semi' (according to the pundits who write in *Steam Railway*) comes from the pre-war description of the locomotives of that class that were 'semi-streamlined', so there we have it. Another name to join the vocabulary of 'Streaks', 'Spam Cans' etc., etc.

Stanier Pacific No. 46239 *City of Chester* on Chester shed in the early 1960s.   *Cleve Jones*

The only event of railway interest that occurred during our main holiday was a trip to Portmadoc and back via Bangor, Caernarvon and Afonwen. The usual 2-6-4T of either Stanier or Fairburn design took us forward from Bangor and as the train ground up the twisting inclines between Penygroes and Pant Glas my dad commented that it was no wonder that Max's 'tankys' were for ever going into the shops for heavy overhauls! (His friend Max Dunn had recently retired as shedmaster at Bangor.) My fascination became aroused on arrival at Afonwen by the presence of a '2251' class Collett locomotive, always rare at Chester. A much more boring (green liveried) class '3' BR 2-6-2T took us forward to Portmadoc where lunch was taken in a High Street café before wandering down to the then somewhat decrepit Harbour station of the Festiniog Railway. A train was making its way along grassy tracks over the Cob pulled by the Fairlie *Earl of Merioneth* then one of only two operational steam locomotives, the 0-4-0ST *Prince* being the other. My dad and I watched in absorbed fascination as the locomotive took water at the end of the platform, ran around its train and then some time later departed along the Cob. We watched as the wisp of exhaust traced its way out of sight across the other side of the estuary up through Minfordd and then made a vow to return as soon as it was practicable for a trip on that most charming of conveyances. Our return trip was punctuated by a somewhat extended wait at Afonwen and I remember with affection the homely warmth of the refreshment rooms on the island platform; there was an excellent choice of cakes on display! I believe that particular establishment was run privately by a lady from the nearby village.

Summer 1963 was to bring the first of the 'adventure' holidays that were to be the hallmark of the next few years. By adventure I mean that just myself and my dad would embark on a trip with only a large knapsack to hold our clothes and apart from our first class train tickets there would be no hotels/guesthouses being booked in advance. We planned that year's trip, which was to be of one week's duration, with the help of my dad's friend Joe Shervington who had experience of the far North of Scotland. It was to include a climb to the summit of Ben Nevis, a trip to the Isle of Skye and onwards to Thurso and Wick, returning via Inverness and the Highland line. We set off on the 'Mail' from Chester to Crewe where a two hour wait was rewarded by my witnessing the activities on Crewe station over the midnight period. An endless procession of mail trains came and went, the bustle on the mail loading platforms had to be seen to be believed. Nearly every train, by then almost all were diesel-hauled, contained only mailvans, many comprising 10 coaches or more! Our Glasgow-bound train arrived at about 12.45 am and we ensconced ourselves in an empty 1st class compartment. The journey north was uneventful; after glimpsing a crowded Dallam (Warrington) shed I slept until well north of Carlisle. We arrived thoroughly weary and bedraggled at Glasgow Central at an indecently early hour not knowing where to go next. A burly ticket collector mumbled something about Buchanan Street, then called us back and apologized and proffered Queen Street as the more likely alternative if we wanted to get to Fort William!

We eventually located the latter, North British, terminus which had a delightfully welcome and cozy café serving an equally welcoming breakfast which was duly consumed after ablutions were done with. Like the west coast main line, steam had also all but disappeared from passenger rosters on the North British. I have to concede that not one journey on this circuitous holiday was to be steam-hauled except for the out and back journeys between Chester and Crewe, where a class '5' obliged on both occasions. Our train was due to depart at 10.00 am and the rear of the train was graced with a 'Beaver Tail' observation car, late of ex-LNER 'Coronation Scot' fame. After a charming journey that seemed to take up the entire day we arrived in Fort William. There was, fortuitously, a tourist information office right outside the station and on making enquiries as to a suitable (cheap) hostelry we were promptly directed to a house about ¼ mile away uphill at the back of the town. This transpired to be a very unimposing semi-detached council house but the landlady exuded West Highland bonhomie and we were duly shown to our comfortable room. As we left the hallway I couldn't help noticing a large brass bell mounted on the wall above the front door but resisted the temptation to enquire as to its purpose! After a welcome evening meal we departed to explore the environs of Fort William. It was a balmy evening so we decided to cross the road to a public footpath and, surmounting the stile, we ascended a steep knoll from where we could get a superb view overlooking the town and Loch Linnhe and the eastern reaches of Loch Eil running west from the head of the former inlet.

Below and to the right of where we stood was the junction of the Mallaig and Glasgow branches of the West Highland line and in the fork the steam shed stood forlorn and empty of locomotives save for one unusual specimen, a Fowler '4F' with tender cab. Brightly painted in a gaudy pinkish red, it stood out of steam in the yard with a large snow plough adorning its front end. That, believe it or not, was the only steam locomotive that I saw north of Glasgow during our entire holiday tour!

We retraced our steps down to the town with gravity assisting us all the way back to the station. As many a rail traveller of yesteryear will recall the track continued past the end of the main platform at Fort William station and on across the road to a looped siding beside the lake (loch) wall. It was here that coaches comprising part of the train that had borne us all the way from Glasgow Queen Street had been parked for the night, clearly ready for the morning return working. I assume the remainder had been worked forward to Mallaig by the same loco that had brought us thus far. Well after a short time exploring the small town our weary travellers retired to their hostelry so as to be ready for the next day, the underlying reason for the journey ... the ascent of Ben Nevis!

Some time in the early hours of the next day we were awoken suddenly by the loud incessant ringing of an electric bell. There was some commotion downstairs, voices on the telephone, doors shutting and then the ringing thankfully ceased. I promptly returned to my slumbers; when I awoke my dad had already dressed and was about to go out in search of his *Daily Mail* before breakfast. When I joined him in the dining room the landlady was explaining and apologizing for the previous night's commotion. Apparently the lady's husband was a volunteer in the local fire brigade and the bell had rung to summon him to the fire station as a fire had been reported in a hunting lodge some 30 miles distant in the area beyond Loch Shiel. He returned home later that afternoon and reported that the place had burnt down by the time they got there ... not surprising really!

Having had a full Scottish breakfast we announced that we were assaulting Ben Nevis that day, our lady was aghast! 'Your no going up the Ben today!', she exclaimed in a manner that didn't brook argument, 'Have ye no seen the mist?'

We countered that the climb was the *raison d'etre* of our trip. She wouldn't hear of it and promptly suggested that if we wanted to live to enjoy the rest of our holiday we should make for Mallaig and take a boat trip across to Skye! So crestfallen we headed for the station once more and caught the morning train to the said coastal fishing port. Many steam fans will have enjoyed that excellent journey in recent years but for us it was the 'slap-snore' of the then ubiquitous Sulzer type '2' that heralded our climbs around the glens that day. We got our boat trip across to Skye, a lift on a fishing smack that dropped us of on dry land at the head of Loch Scavaig after what seemed an endless journey of pitching and rolling through seas that frequently washed right over the boat bringing fish on board at regular intervals! We along with a handful of hardy travellers were deposited ashore and told that we would be picked up at that same spot in three hours' time. Fortunately the weather had cleared enabling us to make an excursion up to Loch Coruisk a few hundred feet up the valley. I have an enduring memory of the pumice-like surface of the glacial rock that allowed a superbly easy grip on one's walking boots so enabling a mere novice like myself to climb the steepest slopes totally unaided by walking sticks or ropes. After a thoroughly enjoyable afternoon scouting around the rocky inlets we were picked up on time by our trusty fishing boat. Following another rough journey we arrived at Mallaig in time to get the 5.00 pm back to Fort William.

The following morning we breakfasted, packed our ruck sack, bade farewell and arrived at the station in time for the Mallaig train. The weather was better, we could actually see the top of the Ben as the train made its way along the shores of Loch Eil, but time in its honoured fashion had run out and we had to continue our journey northwards. We boarded the island ferry boat at Mallaig and continued uneventfully to Kyle of Lochalsh where after a short wait we boarded the Inverness-bound train (again hauled by a ubiquitous type '2'). With hindsight we should have stayed on the train until it reached its final destination, but as we were intent on reaching Thurso we 'unloaded' at Dingwall, that being the junction with the line to the north! Not a very inspiring place on a wet evening; however, we found a B&B near the station with the intention of getting the first morning train out to the north.

Time has erased the reason for us missing that train but I was just glad that we did as my dad had got it into his head that we could see the sights of Thurso and Wick and be on a train home that evening! I can hear the seasoned traveller sucking in his breath, not a chance! We boarded the 'Orchadian' (type '2'-hauled) an hour or so later than originally intended. It doesn't look far on the map but when you carefully study the route that the railway takes, it is far from direct with several incursions inland with that final breathtaking trip across the moors of Caithness from Forsinard to Georgemas Junction. I would thoroughly recommend the trip to anyone interested in seeing the sheer loneliness of those little hamlets amongst the bleak openness of the peat moors with just the single track railway threading its way ever northwards. There is just nothing for over 20 miles apart from the tiny hamlet of Altnabreac with its station served by a single track roadway that came in from the south-east and terminated at the station. We eventually hit civilization again at Georgemas Junction where we changed to a two-coach type '2'-hauled shuttle for the final short trip to Thurso. All thoughts of returning that day had long been dispelled as it was now after one o'clock and we had been travelling since about 9.30 that morning. Digs were found near the station and an afternoon coach trip took us to Dunnet Head (the northernmost tip of mainland Britain) followed by an hour's break at John o'Groats before continuing south to Wick and back along the shore of Loch Watten to Thurso.

The following morning we had time to explore the delights of that little Pentland Firth town of Thurso before starting the long trip home, beginning with the return train working that had brought us the previous day. The only event of note on that journey happened when I was taking a stroll along the train to relieve the boredom of sitting in the compartment. It seemed I spent just a little too long passing through the brake van. A nervous guard popped his head out of his cubicle and asked what I wanted, 'Nothing', said I. The guard then proffered an apology with the words, 'You can't be too careful in this business after that train robbery the other week'! (Remember it was 1963.) Arrival at Inverness was at about 5.30 pm in nice time to board the 'Royal Highlander' overnight sleeper, which was already waiting at an adjacent platform. Whilst we possessed first class tickets they didn't entitle us to a sleeping berth so we had to 'slum it' in a first class compartment which filled rapidly along with the rest of the 15-coach train. The last person into the compartment was a rather dour Scottish gentleman replete with tweed jacket and kilt who kept himself to himself for almost the whole journey. Our motive power for the entire journey to Crewe was an English Electric type '4' (later class '40'). We departed on time and I clearly remember seeing pockets of snow on the Cairngorms that sunny August evening as we headed up the bank towards Slochd Summit and Aviemore.

Dinner was duly consumed in the first class restaurant car and by the time we got to Pitlochry the light was fading and we settled in for a fitful night's sleep. I don't remember anything further of note happening until on passing through Wigan at about 2.30 am our Highland gent, peering out into the gloom, proffered his first communication, 'Och it's ae very nice country yee have doun here!' Wigan? My dad laughed about that for months after!

Arrival at Crewe followed at about 3.00 am, charming! We alighted and made our way to the all-night refreshment room on our arrival platform, stepping over recumbent bodies that were strewn all over the passage ways. Having revived myself with a welcome cup of coffee I left my dad dozing on a platform seat and made my way down to the south end of platform 3, where a Stanier class '5' was standing awaiting a green light. In due course the engine moved off and in the quiet darkness that followed I heard a strange snapping or crackling sound that persisted. I lifted my head in the direction of the sound to be taken aback by the sight of sparks jumping down the insulators above where the engine's chimney had stood! If ever there was a reminder of the frightening power within those overhead cables that was it for me! The carbon deposits left by the smoke were sufficient a conductor to allow the 25,000 volts a ready path to earth, the earthing continued but gradually abated after about 20 minutes.

We boarded the first train out to Chester that Saturday morning and got home 'with the milk'. I think it was about 7.00 am when I finally climbed into my bed with the intention of catching up on some lost 'shut eye'! My slumbers were not to last long, however, as we were to join my mother at Llandudno Junction for the second week of our holiday. So around about midday it was back to Chester station for an early afternoon train to the Junction. Our conveyance was a busy Manchester-Llandudno working hauled by a grimy BR Standard class '5' of, if I recall correctly, 26F Patricroft shed. We quickly found seats in a half-full first class compartment near the front of the train and my dad settled down with his *Daily Mail*.

The journey was uneventful until we passed Mostyn when at some point along the sea wall approaching the Point of Ayr Colliery the driver whistled (probably for a gated crossing) and whistled and whistled! In fact the whistling just didn't stop, the shrill cacophony (remember not all of the class '5s' had the chimed whistle of the 'Brits' but something akin to that of a Great Western or LMS Fowler locomotive). By the time we passed Talacre the folk in the train were beginning to suspect that something had gone wrong with numerous dad's and lads sticking their heads out to see what the fuss was about! My dad just sighed and mumbled, 'Whistle's stuck'. When we finally drew to a halt at Prestatyn amid the banshee and people running down the platform with their fingers in their ears in a vain attempt to get away from the incessant din, my dad got up from his seat and alighted onto the platform. When he realised that the driver and fireman were just standing on the platform looking at the problem he decided that he had to intervene. With obvious authority he demanded that the fireman pass him the hammer from their toolbox (a 12 lb. hammer was part of the standard toolkit). Then, in his Sunday best, he climbed up onto the running plate at the front of the locomotive and inched along until he reached the firebox. With perfect precision he took an almighty swing at the offending whistle which at that range must have been deafening him. I didn't hear the impact but I did hear the result ... silence! He climbed down, handed back the hammer and with a perfunctory, 'Don't use it again, get one of the lads at the Junction to look at it' to the by now thankful driver and fireman and having washed his hands, regained his place in the first class compartment and continued with his paper. All in a day's grief to a locomotive shedmaster on his holiday!

Memorable trips out from the 'Junction' that year included another bash at the Bangor-Afonwen-Portmadoc route but this time with a difference. We actually completed the circuit back to the Junction via the then-truncated Festiniog Railway. Double-Fairlie *Earl of Merioneth* hauled us in fine style up to the then terminus at Tan-y-Bwlch, where we alighted and walked down to the Oakley Arms. From here we took a Crosville bus up to Blaenau Ffestiniog North station where a dmu was waiting to take us back to the Junction in time for tea.

A day or two later my father and I tackled Mount Snowdon. An early start was made via Bangor and Caernarvon where we alighted from the Afonwen bound train and caught a bus to Llanberis. We had arranged that we would meet my mother and Nainy at the summit as they would be following on later that morning on the 'Snowdonian' direct to Llanberis and then via the Snowdon

Holiday snaps showing dad and I: in 1963 at John O'Groats and in 1964, Land's End. Notice the customized road signs!

Author's Collection

Mountain Railway to the summit! So we had to get a move on in order to make the rendezvous. We took the main pathway up from the mountain railway station and I remember being captivated by the sounds of the Swiss rack locomotives storming up the mountain on that misty morning. (Some 35 years later the engines were still giving their best when I spent a number of occasions filming them to assist my good friend Norman Jones with his book about the line.) By the time we reached Hebron we could see the wisp of steam revealing the 'Snowdonian' making its way along the valley below towards Llanberis. We were a quarter of a mile from the summit and just beneath the cloud level, when with the aid of my dad's 16x50 binoculars we espied our two matrons alighting from their train at Clogwyn halt for a breather! We arrived at the summit a minute or two after their arrival … not bad eh? At *mon père's* insistence we had packed a change of vests in our knapsack. This being done, plus a short climb with the ladies up to the tumuli on the actual summit to view the swirling mist, we descended to the café for some liquid refreshment and a snack lunch before returning via the next train back to civilization. My one and only trip on the Llanberis-Caernarvon was being taken that day as part of our return journey on the up 'Snowdonian' (hauled as usual by a Bangor Fairburn 2-6-4T), by that time the only passenger working on the line and a seasonal one at that!

Summer 1964 brought a trip to the other end of 'Blighty'. Well having reached John O' Groats in 1963 we had to complete the act the following year! On reflection I now wished we had done the Cornish trip first for by the time we got down there in August 1964, all Western steam had vanished west of Exeter. Indeed the very last ex-GWR '63XX' Mogul I ever saw in normal service was one dirty specimen passing light over the flyover at Cogload Junction near Taunton. We departed Chester at about 8.30 am on a Paddington-bound express hauled by a then brand-new two-tone green diesel Brush type '4' (later class '47'), with brief sightings of panniers at Croes Newydd (Wrexham) then changing at Salop (where an immaculate Salop-based 'Manor' class was espied negotiating the triangle) onto a Manchester-Plymouth express hauled by the same class of diesel. An immaculate 'Hall' was seen at Hereford standing alone in the northbound platform, then a locomotive change was made at Newport where a maroon 'Western' class diesel continued the journey as far as Plymouth. My frustration at the grass banking twixt main line and shed at Severn Tunnel Junction prompted my dad to remark out loud, 'They only put it there to stop you schoolboys from seeing the engines'. Now that embarrassed me no end in the compartment full of stuffy adults!

The best was yet to come when at Bristol Stapleton Road I witnessed a shining No. 7023 *Penrice Castle* standing in the up platform with a Paddington express. She pulled out shortly after we arrived and even though there were only 10 on she stopped on the bank east of the station and 'whistled up' a banker, this was a very clean black '57XX' pannier which had been standing on a slip road outside of the station. The banker ran up to the back of the train and 'crowed' to the 'Castle' which then replied and the whole entourage then started away in fine style, a most memorable sight and one which was very shortly to disappear forever save for re-enactments on our preserved lines of today. On returning to our compartment I quizzed my dad as to the need for a 'Castle' calling up a banker when it was obvious it was more than man enough to handle such a relatively short train. His reply, as one might expect from an LMS man, was somewhat derogatory indicating that Great Western men were 'fussy' and inevitably expected assistance whether it was necessary or not! (A 1953 working timetable shows the maximum unassisted load for a 'Castle' up the 1 in 75 of Filton bank as 420 tons, but, of course, the driver may reduce this depending on the condition of the engine.) Perhaps the thing that stuck in my memory of that day was the fine external condition of most of the ex-GWR engines on main line passenger duties.

Some Southern steam was seen fleetingly at Exeter but once past that point the line was totally barren of steam. I tell a lie! At the back of Laira shed, by then already a modern diesel depot, was stored a forlorn '14XX' auto-tank, painted out in red lead. It was probably one of the engines destined for the fledgling Dart Valley Railway. On arrival at Plymouth North Road our maroon 'Western' was changed for one of the then ubiquitous green 'Warships', this took us forward to our first destination, Penzance. We arrived here weary and hungry at about 6.30 pm. The following week, spent in the 'Duchy', we travelled on the St Ives, Falmouth, Newquay and Looe branches. Apart from St Ives we spent at least one night in each watering hole. Without exception all of the branches were worked by dmus, of course the most esoteric being the Looe branch with its steep drop down from Liskeard and reversal at Coombe Junction, still extant today beneath the lofty Moorswater viaduct carrying the main line above.

Our homeward journey was much the same as the outward one being a mixture of 'Warship', 'Western' and Brush type '4' diesels. There was an exception though, we got steam from Salop to Chester, much to my chagrin not a gleaming 'Hall' or 'County' but a grimy LMS class '5', very much the pattern of things north of Shrewsbury when lines north of Craven Arms fell into London Midland territory after January 1963. I do recall, however, seeing an ex-GWR '56XX' 0-6-2T from Croes Newydd shunting at Chester on our arrival that evening. It has to be said that by late 1964 ex-GWR engines in the Chester area were getting like 'hen's teeth' - rare! I do remember, however, seeing two examples at opposite ends of the appearance spectrum when leaving Chester for Euston early one morning in the October half-term holiday. An immaculate 'Hall' was waiting to enter the station on the Greenford parcels whilst on the ex-LNWR shed stood a contrasting 'Grange' in a very grimy condition indeed!

Hawarden Grammar School Christian Union Trip, 12th to 24th April, 1965

Well if that doesn't sound exciting then what would? The head of religious studies - Mr 'Duffy' Gower had for some months been engaged in the planning of a trip, for willing 5th and 6th form participants, to Guernsey in the coming Easter holiday. As I had never been to the Channel Islands and as I qualified for free rail and sea travel it was too tempting an opportunity to miss! That there might be an underlying hidden agenda to the safari never occurred to this innocent 16 year old! Well the chosen day in April finally arrived and our respective parents ferried us to the rendezvous point, the entrance to Chester General station. In my case a lift to the station was gained courtesy of my pal Michael's father who had something our family didn't have (or need?), a motor car!

Our train was to be the Birkenhead Woodside to Paddington sleeper, departing Chester at 9.30 pm; we had a berth reservation on the outward journey only. Goodbyes to parents being dispensed with we made our collective way through the barrier and over the footbridge to platform 14, then the only bi-directional platform in the station.

Our conveyance duly arrived behind a Birkenhead 'Crab' blowing off and causing great consternation amongst the female element of the party. I distinctly remember my pal's sister Maureen yelling out, 'Oh why do trains always do that?' While the Mogul unhooked and a grumbling Brush type '4' diesel backed down onto the western end of the train, we concentrated on settling in our allotted berths, the thrill of it all … never had the privilege of travelling in a sleeper before! Departure was on time and progress as I recall was necessarily lazy. (My dad later remarked that he and mum had made the short walk from home to the green overlooking Saltney Junction to wave as the train went by, but as we were in a sleeper with the berth windows on the offside of the train we missed them.) After Gobowen I think I turned in only to be woken up by an engine working hard on a passing freight when we spent an inordinately long time in Birmingham Snow Hill. Paddington, where a brief sighting of the only steam visible, a '94XX' pannier on station shunt duties, was reached at an unearthly hour and we were allowed to remain on board until 7.00 am. Bleary-eyed, we assembled at the concourse end of the arrival platform before taking the 'tube' to Waterloo for the commencement of the next part of our journey. Things got more interesting here, steam haulage of the Weymouth boat train by one of Nine Elms' named BR class '5s' nonetheless! I can't be sure but I think we had No. 73082 *Camelot*. Departure was at 8.10 am prompt and no sooner had we got underway when a most welcome breakfast of bacon and eggs etc. was served we all had reserved seats in the restaurant car, not even first class. Halycon days looking back, no queuing at a buffet counter for a microwaved bacon bap in a packet! Well that's progress as they say. I distinctly remember seeing a pristine ex-GWR 'Hall' outside Basingstoke shed but can't recall its exact identity.

On arrival at Weymouth things got really interesting as our class '5' was replaced by an 0-6-0 diesel shunter for that much renowned tortuous journey through the winding streets down to the harbour station where our BR ship, the MV *Sarnia*, was waiting alongside the quay. That journey down the street tramway was halted at least twice by offending motorists who had placed their cars too near to the tracks, or within the white demarcation lines that parallelled the single line. One could almost lean out of the windows at the end of the carriages and touch the buildings on the bends as, with flanges squealing, we drifted by at a near walking pace. The island platform buildings still in their Great Western hue of brown and cream eventually came alongside as did the BR blue hull of our ship. Embarkation, despite the clutter on the platform of passengers and their baggage was relatively swift and soon we were on our way across the Channel towards our destination, some four hours or so sailing time away. Everything appeared to be going well with the majority in high spirits until at some point in mid-channel a bit of a swell got up and suddenly most of the female contingent disappeared in the direction of the ladies. Not a good move as pretty soon most were out on deck gasping for fresh air!

British Railways 204 bhp diesel-mechanical shunter No. D2082 awaits its next duty on Weymouth Quay tramway on the 4th May, 1963.   *C.L. Caddy*

MV *Caesarea* enters St Peter Port, Guernsey in April 1965.   *Author*

Personally my pal and I enjoyed the whole spectacle but nevertheless were glad to arrive at Saint Peter Port late that afternoon.

By 1965 there were no railways on Guernsey save for the bus company called the 'Guernsey Railway Co.' This was comprised of a fleet of bright green Bedford 'OBs' that ran over much of the island with the name of the company emblazoned boldly on their sides. They were born out of the electric tramway that ran north from the capital to St Sampson's, a distance of about three miles. Before that a standard gauge steam railway existed from 1879; this became the an electric tramway in 1891 and operated until 1934 when it was closed and replaced with a fleet of motor buses that rapidly spread its size and route tentacles over much of the island.

Come 24th April we had been all well and truly immersed in the ways of righteousness by our well meaning mentor and thus departed on the sister ship of our outward conveyance, the *Caesarea*. The sea journey must have been without issue. On arrival at Weymouth we were once again herded onto the Waterloo-bound boat train and after that delightful return through the streets to Weymouth Town station we were coupled up to an unrebuilt 'Spam Can'. This time we had a compartment filled with equal numbers of lads and lasses, and sat intently listening to my pal Mike reciting extracts from the then best selling paperback *The Carpetbaggers*; so much for the efforts of 'Duffy' Gower! On arrival at Waterloo the identity of our 'Spam Can' was revealed as No. 34006 *Bude*. Our return from Paddington to Chester was again by the down Birkenhead sleeper. However, as this time I didn't qualify for a berth I used my first class pass to obtain an empty compartment. We took the long route via Reading and Didcot and I don't recall waking until the train was running through Saltney yard.

Following the pattern of the previous two years, the summer 1965 holiday was to commence with my father and I doing our own thing for the first week. First port of call was to be Southend-on-Sea, more of a trip back in time for my dad as he and his brother Arthur had spent a couple of years at Westcliffe-on-Sea after their mother had died around 1910. He hadn't been back since and thought that a couple of days spent sampling the delights of the 'Kursaal', the longest pier, *et al*, would impress young 'Robbo' … well it didn't! To be honest I don't think my dad was too impressed either, what impressed one as an eight-year-old in an earlier more rustic age wasn't going to work that magic again. For one thing the 'Tilbury Tanks' had long since been replaced by more mundane electric-multiple-units (emu), not to mention the three-cylinder Stanier 2-6-4Ts somewhere in between. Of course the resort had also lost most of its turn of the century charm.

We retraced our steps to the grand metropolis via Fenchurch Street and then made our way via Waterloo to East Horsley near Guildford, a charming wooded village well and truly in the stockbroker belt of Surrey. It was here that my dad's brother and sisters had set up home after retiring and I have to say I took to the place and its affluence impressed me. It had a charming station on the old London & South Western Railway (LSWR) line from Surbiton to Guildford via Effingham Junction and on some mornings one could watch a Bulleid 'Q1' class 0-6-0 from the nearby Guildford (70C) shed shunting in the adjacent goods yard. All passenger workings by then, of course, were handled by the green emus. After a couple of days spent at this watering hole over, we made our way back to Waterloo, there to catch another emu this time to Portsmouth. Here we crossed

In August 1965 we landed at Ryde Pier whereupon we elected to walk down the pier to the town for a meal. Halfway along the pier we were passed by the train pictured here. With a bit more prescence of mind I could have included the tram running alongside in the shot, but it was always going to be there wasn't it?   *Author*

Later we took a train from Ryde to Ventnor where we arrived at this charming terminus hidden away in a chalk pit above the town. This 1959 view shows Adams 'O2' class 0-4-4-T No. 16 *Ventnor* waiting to depart into the long tunnel that will bring it and its train out into the sunshine at Wroxall. The engine's Westinghouse pump and air reservoir are prominent in this picture.

J.M. Bentley

over to another of my dad's old stamping grounds, the Isle of Wight. Our ferry was one of those quaint old LSWR paddle boats that just didn't look right with its gaudy blue hull and 'barbed wire' logo on the red funnel! Arrival at Ryde was to reveal that wonderful anachronistic railway that in those days was pretty well intact save for a couple of the more remote outlying branches that had been axed some years previously. We decided to make Ventnor our base and so boarded a train at the town station for that place which was then the furthest one could get on the system. What a wonderful experience, those delightful vintage carriages pulled by one of a fleet of ex-LSWR Adams 'O2' 0-4-4 tank engines, ours sporting the name *Ningwood* (No. 18). My most memorable experience on that first journey was the long claustrophobic single line tunnel that preceded our arrival at Ventnor. The station here was sited in a chalk excavation right at the top of the town. There were three platform faces, a single platform and an island platform separated by a single road between them. Access across this line, to and from the island platform, was by a portable ship-style gangway. This was removable, to allow the engine to run around its train via a turntable, should it have drawn into the single line twin platform road.

We spent the remainder of the week at Ventnor and using a modest guest house near the seafront as our base set off each day to explore different parts of the island, initially by the then less-truncated railway network than one finds there today. Our first journey was to dad's old stamping ground of Shanklin, where we found a rather intriguing 'show' in progress on the pier. This was entitled the 'Green Ray Machine' and invited the uninitiated to take part in 'disappearing' before the eyes of the audience. Who got volunteered for the experience? No prizes for guessing! So in the darkened auditorium I was ushered up onto the stage to be placed via a rear door in a small triangular booth that had a mirror on one of its rear walls. The front wall had a window in it out of which our nail-biting audience could see the upper half of my torso. The lights dimmed, a green light came on somewhere above my head, and the audience went oooh and ahh! All except my dad that is, who started laughing! I turned around and there I was in the mirror as before! Lights came up, everyone clapped and the man let me out of the booth. I sat and watched the next contestant go through the experience, when the lights dimmed and when the 'Green Ray' appeared the contestant simply disappeared!

Another day saw us taking a trip down to Cowes via Newport, a neat little two-platform terminus greeted our arrival at our destination. The one enduring memory I have of Cowes was watching the flagship Cunard liner RMS *Queen Elizabeth* leaving Southampton Water and opening up her turbines as she headed for Cherbourg prior to the Atlantic crossing. Pity that unlike the *Queen Mary* she came to such an ignominious end in Hong Kong harbour some years later. Our trip to Cowes meant that we had then traversed the whole of the then extant Isle of Wight railway system. Little memory remains of the journey home, save that I recall seeing an ex-GWR 'Hall' on Fratton shed which probably worked through from Western Region rails via Salisbury on a weekend special. We spent some time taking photographs of the rapidly disappearing Euston; by that time demolition of the old LNWR buildings was well advanced, the Great Hall having already disappeared. Our return north was courtesy of one of the newly-installed blue electrics, at Crewe we changed and were steam-hauled back to Chester.

The end of 1965 was something of a personal milestone as far as rail travel was concerned. By then I was apprenticed to Hawker Siddeley Aviation's Chester factory and therefore no longer qualified for free first class travel courtesy of my father. My first 'paying' journey was from Chester to Colwyn Bay on Christmas Eve with my parents who of course journeyed on to Llandudno Junction. Our train rolled in to Chester's platform 4 behind a Stanier class '5', the stock was also by that time truly vintage comprising period II and III vehicles. I alone alighted 'early' at Colwyn Bay - that was to be my final steam-hauled experience on BR. My reason for getting off at Colwyn Bay was so that I could collect a model kit that I had promised myself (with Christmas money) from that doyen of the white metal kit makers, GEM Models of Rhos on Sea. On arrival at the GEM shop counter I was greeted by none other than George Mellor himself. My request for the newly-launched LNWR 'Prince of Wales' was duly addressed and I distinctly remember Mr Mellor relating that the last time he had seen one of these locomotives it was shunting at Abergele in 1949. This was to be my second LNWR 'OO' gauge white metal kit as my father and I had put together a 'K's' 'Coal Tank' early the previous year.

The Christmas break was to prove uneventful save for one abiding memory. On Boxing Day my father and I set out on one of our long time favourite walks. From the Junction we crossed the Cob to Conway and proceeding initially by the Sychnant Pass road we climbed to the summit of Conway Mountain. I couldn't put my finger on it but there was something strange about my dad that day. He was sullen and non-communicative, completely lacking in the customary enthusiasm that he always displayed for life when out walking in one of his favourite haunts.

Euston station with rebuilding in progress in August 1965. What a mess ... and it didn't look much better when it was finished either!   *Author*

Chapter Ten

Friends and Colleagues

John Maxwell Dunn M.I.LocoE. 1898-1969

My father was not by any description what one would call a gregarious man, if anything he shunned the limelight (if such a thing ever fell on the occupants of a locomotive shed). He made few lasting friends throughout his life and those that he did make, he invariably kept. One such was Maxwell Dunn, like my father he was an LNWR apprentice, with time served at Willesden shed. He was, though, a few years older and to some extent, in the early years at least, took the young Jack Robinson under his wing. Max was a 'dyed in the wool' railway enthusiast and it was this similar quality that he recognized in my father. He lived in nearby Wood Green and was the son of a London furrier who along with his wife had given the young Max a somewhat 'indulged' upbringing as he was an only child. His passion for all things LNWR is well chronicled in his reminiscences *Reflections on a Railway Career* published by Ian Allan in 1966. Indeed latter day enthusiasts have a lot to thank Max Dunn for, as very few of his ilk made the effort to chronicle their career experiences in the way he did. Unfortunately for Max he did so in a somewhat 'warts and all' way which made him very unpopular with a number of his contemporaries. Indeed if his writings are to be believed, and there is no reason to disbelieve them, he had every reason to relate his experiences in the way that he chose.

However, it is not for the likes of myself to pass either judgment or comment on the moral issues of the life and career of Maxwell Dunn. What I can pass comment on is my own experiences of the man and the influences he had over my immediate family and my own early years and career choices. As already mentioned he began his career at Willesden leaving school in Wood Green in the summer of 1913 and starting under the auspices of the London area district locomotive superintendent Francis Dingley, a colleague, neighbour and close friend of my grandfather John Robinson. From an early age Max loved railways and having sampled, as a small child, the experience of seeing one of the Webb three-cylinder Compounds replete with its frontal 'half moon' arriving at Euston, his affinities became more and more 'North Western' as he grew up. Although chronicled in his book, he took great delight in regaling me with this particular yarn during a long and most memorable weekend that I spent at his Sussex abode with him and his wife Sally back in the late summer of 1966. I think even back in those days he considered that he must have been one of the only men still then alive to have sampled this visual experience! There used to be a monthly story in the *Reader's Digest* where readers were invited to describe their 'most unforgettable character', in my case that character would most definitely have been Maxwell Dunn. Some contemporaries had described him as being something of an eccentric; to my mind he liked people to believe this, but in truth he was a very astute man who liked to divorce himself from the modern world. He admitted to me that he felt that he had been born 50 years too late. He never read newspapers or listened to the 'wireless news' and a television had never been allowed to enter his household. There were periods of his life that he just would not discuss and he had an abhorrence of all things aeronautical. One of his regular chants, if questioned about this, would be answered by, 'If God wanted man to fly, he would have given him wings!' In his hall hat stand stood a fine looking stout round-handled walking stick which he always used and referred to as his 'propeller'.

He had a convoluted sense of humour, whilst all who encountered the stick knew what he called it, few really knew that it was indeed cut from the blade of a real propeller courtesy of a crashed Sopwith 'Camel' that he encountered whilst serving in the Royal Flying Corps at Caffiers in Northern France in 1918! I got this from my dad, nobody could coax the 'best forgotten' military experiences of serving in the 'War to end all wars' from Max. His servitude was nevertheless thankfully short, coming near the end of hostilities and necessarily after the end of his apprenticeship. On returning to Willesden in 1919 he befriended my dad who as related earlier had commenced his apprenticeship at the London shed in May 1919. During his time at Willesden, Max, who was studying mechanical engineering by correspondence course (there was no day release to attend 'Tech' in those days), was asked if he would consider presenting a paper to the Institution of Locomotive Engineers. In due course he compiled a thesis on locomotive blast pipe design and presented the paper during a meeting of the Institution members at Caxton Hall in November 1917. This was later published in the 'Proceedings of the Institution' and the *Railway Gazette*. As a direct result he gained associated membership of that august body that in 1971 became the Railway Division of the Institution of Mechanical Engineers. It was to become a thorn in the side of many of his future superiors that he held that coveted qualification! Indeed my father envied him that, but moved away from the influence of the 'educated elite' of the locomotive world when he relocated to North Wales at the end of his apprenticeship.

My father always referred to him as 'Max the Scribe'. It is to my regret that my dad wasn't more like him as this tome would have been so much the easier to write if he too had recorded his professional anecdotes in the same way. But in fairness my dad was an excellent draughtsman which is something JMD was not. I have several of Max's 'sketches', for that is what one can best call them, of locomotive parts that he, like my dad, used in the mutual improvement classes - they just don't compare with the accuracy and detail of *mon père's* efforts! The other area that Max excelled in was that of recording his daily experiences on camera. His large collection of negatives* was carefully indexed and used judicially in his various and regularly published periodical writings as well as in 'Reflections'.

If ever there was a man who had the courage of his convictions then he was certainly that man! Throughout his career he seemed to revel in treading on the toes of 'incompetent authority', that is to say those above, who in his estimation fell short of their self-perceived importance, value and ability. He made a very risky start to his career when in 1919 he elected to ignore the masses going on a railway strike and took turns at firing on some of the limited 'management run' services between Bletchley and Euston. When the strike was over so was his

---

* The collection is now held in the archives of the LNWR Society and prints are available from the photographic officer.

career at Willesden shed, he hardly dare show his face . After a meeting with Francis Dingley he was made to 'disappear', that was the start of his tenure in South Wales. His career experiences have been well documented, but for the sake of the many who have not had the chance to read 'Reflections' I will briefly go over the progress of his career and relate a few of the more memorable and amusing anecdotes.

He started at Abergavenny ('a very pleasant town') in November 1919 and among the stories worth relating is the one where one evening just before 'knocking off' Max decided to move a 'MM' class 2-8-0 (the LNWR version of J.G. Robinson 'ROD') still in steam, to a wheel drop position ready for working on the following morning, whilst in the darkness inside the shed. In his own words he came close to demolishing Abergavenny gas works which stood to the rear of the shed building. Not realizing that the engine was fitted with a 'train only' Westinghouse air brake system that was linked to the regulator, and to stop the engine he needed to apply the steam brake, the engine started to move and the regulator could not be closed as the header discharge valve was coupled to it! Fortunately one of the other fitters realized what was happening and leaping up onto the footplate grabbed the steam brake stopping the engine, but not before a lot of banging up of wheels, etc., had taken place! The ensemble came to rest up against the planing machine which was within an inch or two of the rear wall of the shed. Although no trace of the shed exists today a very nice bronze plaque depicting an LNWR 0-6-2 'Coal Tank' has been placed on the old wall that ran alongside the line from the 'Brecon Road' overbridge near the shed's entrance. On the plaque are to be found the words, 'Near this spot stood the local engine sheds which once housed nearly one hundred steam engines'. A fitting memorial to that most tortuous of ex-LNWR lines, the 'Heads of the Valleys' line from Abergavenny to Merthyr and to that most typical of the line's workhorses, the Webb 'Coal Tank'. Today the old trackbed is occupied by the new by-pass road and whilst passing through a few years ago I stopped to photograph what remains of the old LNWR. The bridge (now replaced by a modern concrete road bridge) over the River Usk reminded me of one of Max's tales of how on the nightshift an engine, occasionally a 'Super D' with some unusual items in the tender, would often 'sneak' out from the shed and gaining the main line would trundle off down to the (then girder) bridge where it would stop. Shortly after that there would come the sounds of heavy articles 'splooshing' into the murky depths below, scrap and redundant firebars, axle boxes, broken springs and lord knows what would be quietly 'got rid of' before the culprit trundled quietly back to the shed!

There are many amusing anecdotes of his sojourn in South Wales to be found in his book, 'Reflections'. However, there is one that isn't and that is about the time he took his one and only evening trip down to Cardiff from Tredegar (where he had moved to after his spell at Abergavenny) via Newport. He intended to return by the Rhymney Railway, this would entail a walk over the hill from Rhymney to Tredegar at the end of his journey, but would allow him to depart much later in the evening than by the outward route. On returning to the said railway's station in Cardiff in time to catch the last train home, he found the place all in darkness save for one platform which was still lit. Apart from

Above: Abergavenny (Brecon Road) station in LMS days.   *N.H. Lee/LNWR Society Collection*

Below: Abergavenny shed taken from the road bridge *circa* 1925.   *J.M. Dunn*

Top right: A January 1958 view from within the by then, closed shed at Abergavenny. On the right is the Brecon Road No. 2 signal box.   *N.H. Lee/LNWR Society Collection*

Bottom right: This plaque is mounted on a wall adjacent to the site of the former engine shed at Abergavenny, now part of the town's bypass. The wording beneath the 'Coal Tank' reads: 'Near this spot stood the local engine sheds which once housed nearly one hundred steam engines'.
                                                                            Author

some activity in the adjacent goods yard, little seemed to be happening, then all went quiet and the platform lights went out. Max became a little alarmed at this and went to the booking office to enquire about the expected train. 'It's gone' came the reply, 'But I've been standing here for the last half-hour and I haven't seen a train!' exclaimed our intrepid traveller. 'But the last train always departs from the goods yard', came the infuriating reply. Needless to say he never attempted to go to Cardiff and back of an evening again!

One can speculate as to why he made an evening trip to Cardiff, perhaps the most obvious thought that comes to mind is a visit to see a lady friend; somehow I doubt it. Max was never one to make an issue over matters concerning the opposite sex, let alone go chasing many miles in pursuit of its members. Around the time he worked at Tredegar it is believed in my family that he met his wife to be, a young lady who seems to have had great attachment to her mother and hailing from the village near Abergavenny that was the first station out of that town - Govilon. I remember Sally Dunn as a short lady with more than a passing knowledge of things 'railway', no surprises there! She had a somewhat off-putting demeanour and greeted you with a 'scowl' but once engaged in conversation she would transform into a lovely lady who in my precious memory was a truly superb cook, being able, like so many 'impoverished' railway wives of her day, to rustle up the most delightful meal from very little in the way of culinary materials. With the passing of the years Max came to sport something of a 'corporation' that was testimony to her expertise in the kitchen. Their marriage was, as I believe, a somewhat hurried affair with minimal guest attendance save for the necessary witnesses. No offspring were forthcoming and Max held a well-heralded distaste for all small children, be it their own or their parents' fault for any misbehaviour!

After spending some seven years at Tredegar he moved on to Blaenavon shed where he spent a further seven years before leaving South Wales for good on being promoted to the position of foreman fitter at Llandudno Junction in 1935. Here, of course, he was re-united with his old friend Jack Robinson, who by then was 10 years into his servitude as a fitter at 7A. Much has been chronicled in 'Reflections' about his time spent at that shed and the frequent 'run-ins' he had with the 'powers that be'. Chief protagonist by all accounts (including that of my father) was of course the resident district locomotive superintendent Mr J.T. King, who it would seem disliked Max despite his slavish conscientiousness and total dedication to getting things right at that shed! Reading between the lines I think it was more a case of professional jealousy than anything else. However, it must be said that Max had an uncanny knack of 'making his efforts known' to those in the locomotive running departments at Crewe and above. I think his membership of the 'Locomotive Engineers' and his regular attendance at the various meetings and works visits put him touch with 'those that mattered', hence the professional jealousy amongst his immediate superiors.

It was whilst at that shed that he became a friend of the family in a more rounded sense as both he and Sally became firm friends of my mother and my elder sister Ann who was but a small child at that time. My father had a devilish sense of humour and, knowing that Max had a fascination for the supernatural, suggested after a meal one Christmas time, when they were all sitting around the table playing cards, that they indulge in a little experiment with the occult! He suggested that they try the age-old 'game' called 'The Spirit Moves'. This is the one where everyone seated around a table puts their hands on the edges of it and invites the 'spirit' of a known deceased to move the table upwards. Well everyone laid on their hands and after a short interlude the table started to rise and Max got quite hysterical it seems! My dad couldn't control himself any longer and burst out laughing, giving the game away - he had the table carefully balanced on his knees! I would guess Max forgave the humiliation and took the 'prank' as just another example of my father's 'impish' sense of humour.

Max moved to what was to be his final position in 1944 having accepted a promotion to the position of shed master at Bangor. His days there are well chronicled in his memoirs and often my father would answer his phone at Mold Junction to be greeted by Max regaling him with a tale of yet another 'run-in'. Advice from *mon père* to accept things as they were, were seldom heeded and during his time at Bangor Max made many enemies both above and below himself. Having said that he instilled in his men a pride in their jobs and was, if somewhat autocratic, well respected by the younger fitters and their apprentices. When visiting other sheds, notably Llandudno Junction to see the district locomotive superintendent, he might, for example, call upon a lad in the shed yard to readily identify a component of an engine's motion. If the unlucky recipient of his enquiry was unable to give a ready answer he might be further interrogated about other parts of the locomotive in question!

In those early years (for me) at Llandudno Junction, Max and Sally were regular visitors and he was known as 'Uncle Max' by both my sister and I. As mentioned earlier he had a singular dislike of children, probably brought on from his own childhood and schooldays of which little is mentioned in his reminiscences save for the time he won the form prize for an essay about

Ex-LNWR Webb 'Coal Tank' 0-6-2T No. 58903 stands with its motor train in the Bethesda bay at Bangor in 1950. *J.M. Dunn*

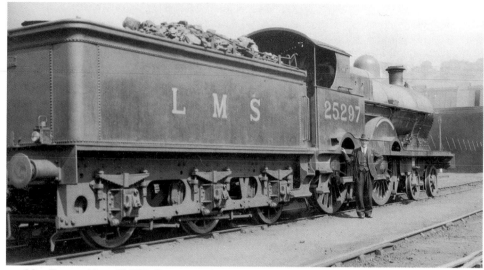

Max Dunn with ex-LNWR 'Precursor' class 4-4-0 No. 25297 *Sirocco* at Bangor shed. In all 130 'Precursors' were built between 1904 and 1907. *Sirocco* remained in traffic until 1948, it was the last of the class to be withdrawn and the only one to make it to nationalization, although it never carried the British Railways number (58010) that it had been allocated.

J.P. Richards/LNWR Society

Max Dunn stands next to the tender of 'Royal Scot' class 4-6-0 No. 6154 *The Hussar* which has 'gone on the floor' at the entrance to Bangor tunnel *circa* 1946.   *J.P. Richards/LNWR Society*

railways. When he realized that I was 'a chip off the old block' he became interested in my scholastic progress. In early 1965 when I was planning on leaving school and seeking an engineering apprenticeship, he wrote a testimonial on the strict understanding that I would not use it to secure a job on British Railways! Such was his total dislike by that time of anything to do with the said 'institution' of British Railways. This also came with a stern warning to dress correctly for an interview and 'use the Queen's English'. That testimonial helped to secure for me offers of an engineering apprenticeship at both Rolls Royce Aero Engines, Derby and the then De Havilland division of Hawker Siddeley Aviation at Chester, subject to obtaining the necessary 'O' level GCEs in the 1965 examinations.

To Whom it may concern.   11th.February,1965.

ANTHONY JOHN ROBINSON.

I have much pleasure in stating that I have known ANTHONY JOHN ROBINSON all his life - his father and I have been friends for over forty-five years - and can testify that he has been well brought-up, is honest and able to concentrate, of a courteous and pleasant disposition and of good appearance and address.

He is at present in the fifth form at Hawarden Grammar School and his interests include farming, cycling, model engineering and engineering drawing.

J.M.Dunn.
(Late Locomotive Shed Master,
British Railways, Bangor.)

Max Dunn poses next to the first Ivatt class '2' 2-6-2T No. 41200 at Bangor in 1952. This proved to be a very popular engine.   *W.G. Rear*

He retired in 1958 (early - aged 60) and one of his first successes was to secure from scrapping the ex-LNWR 'Coal Tank No. 1054 (BR No. 58926), this being retired from the Abergavenny-Merthyr line that same year. He petitioned all of his friends (having been petitioned himself by one of his pals - Geoffrey Platt a well-known LNWR enthusiast) inside and outside the industry and some influential people who were LNWR enthusiasts. The locomotive, having first found a home at the Hednesford depot of the Railway Preservation Society, eventually (in 1964) found its way into the arms of the National Trust's Penrhyn Castle Museum as one of its earliest exhibits. Today we LNWR enthusiasts have much to thank Max Dunn for: he was directly responsible for the preservation of one of only five* standard gauge locomotives from what was once one of the largest locomotive stables that the world has ever known!

In an earlier chapter mention was made of a visit that my father and I made to Bangor shed in October 1957. The journey was made from Llandudno

_____

* The five standard gauge LNWR survivors are:

2-2-2 *Cornwall* - originally designed by John Ramsbottom but much modified by F.W. Webb.

2-4-0 'Precedent' class *Hardwicke*, famous for its record run in the hands of Ben Robinson in August 1895. These engines once very common were generally known as 'Jumbos' and designed by F.W. Webb.

0-6-2 'Coal Tank' No. 1054.

0-8-0 'Super D' ('G2') No. 49395, much modified by C.J. Bowen Cooke from the original 'G' class. Subsequently (by the LMS) fitted with a Belpaire firebox and reduced height cab roof for the Midland loading gauge.

0-4-0 'Ramsbottom Tank', an early small shunting locomotive that was saved as it spent most of its final years in private industrial ownership.

Junction as one of a number of days out during the autumn half-term break. At the time the old LNWR 'north light' shed roof was being removed in readiness for the replacement BR design that can still be seen today. We were met by the shed master himself as we alighted from our train and were led across the sleeper crossing between the lines of locomotives and into the shed which was then largely roofless. The short journey was fraught with hazards as men were working above us, bits of masonry and timber were making frequent trips to earth and no such things as 'hard hats' were available for shed staff let alone visitors! On gaining his office Max immediately arranged for refreshments in the way of three mugs of shed tea. As one might expect his office was a veritable Aladdin's den of railway paraphernalia. Whilst the walls were adorned with a collection of framed photographs, mainly of early LNWR types, there were at least two large framed drawings, one showing a sectioned Webb 'Coal Tank' and another depicting a sectioned Fowler '4F'. Pride of place went to a superbly detailed scale (½ in. to the foot) model of the original (No. 1400) Webb 4-6-0 'Bill Bailey' built in cardboard apparently by a 16-year-old. This was displayed in a glass case on the mantelpiece opposite his desk. The model, which had working inside Joy's valve gear, was presented to him by a person unknown back in 1952 in order to save it from being 'ill treated' at the hands of children. My father and Max always got on famously and were both devotees of the old LNWR, most of their discussions being about their common experiences with the locomotives of that long gone company.

At the end of that afternoon we walked to Max's home in upper Bangor where we met up with Sally who had prepared one of her delightful meals in anticipation of our visit. After dinner dad and Max continued with their reminiscing whilst I was allowed to 'play' with one of Max's models; this time a much more robustly made Bassett Lowke 'O' gauge clockwork 4-4-0 'George the Fifth' (*see photograph on page 138*). Compared with my tinplate clockwork Hornby 'O' gauge stuff back home this was a terrific engine, remember I was only eight going on nine at the time. Even so I don't think pushing it up and down the hearth did it much good! The owner didn't seem to mind, though, and encouraged me in my interest of steam engines.

Max committed to paper his own philosophy on how to successfully manage an engine shed:

> During my tenure of office at Bangor shed I had endeavoured, with I am pleased to say a good deal of success, to innoculate a spirit of enthusiasm among all sections of the staff and in doing so I issued to the foreman written 'Hints on the handling of Staff at a Running Shed'. As these may possibly be of interest I give them herewith.
>
> 1. Bear in mind that a Running Shed is not like a factory where work can be kept up at a steady pace for the full turn of duty. There are 'rush' periods and 'slack' periods.
> 2. Cultivate the art of being 'Boss' without making everybody aware of the fact.
> 3. Always say 'please' and 'thank you' especially when dealing with subordinates. The lower down the ladder the person addressed, the more polite one should be.
> 4. If you have asked any members of the staff to be 'on their mettle' for any particular occasion and things have gone off well, don't forget to be as careful to thank each one of them as you were to ask for their co-operation.

5. Be friendly without being familiar and do not allow anyone to take liberties. Learn how to 'freeze' if necessary.

6. Do not pass jocular remarks unless you are prepared to accept something similar in return.

7. When giving an instruction always start off with 'Will you … ? in preference to 'Go and do so and so'.

8. Never give an instruction that anyone can legitimately refuse to carry-out. It can easily result in what a Chinaman calls 'loss of face' or, in plain English, loss of prestige which is to be avoided at all costs.

9. If you want something done which is not in strict accordance with Rules and Regulations put the request to the party concerned in a very discreet way.

10. If you have an engine to dispose of and re-prepare or any other job that has to be done in a hurry by all means grace the proceedings with your presence - it will do all the good in the world - BUT

   (a) Hold your tongue.
   (b) Do not interfere.
   (c) Resist all temptation to do some of the work yourself.

11. Remember that the MORE you know, the LESS you know.

12. Learn the value of a 'blind eye' and how to use it.

13. Remember there is no virtue in work for work's sake.

14. Do not find fault unnecessarily. If you must, remember that a 'ticking-off' administered in a semi-jocular manner can be very effective and often more so than a stern 'telling-off'.

I do not suppose the foregoing would meet with the approval of the modernizers, work-studiers (who work-studies the work-studiers?!) and efficiency-mongers but they paid in the days when railwaymen felt it was a privilege to belong to a deep-rooted organization on which the public depended with almost as much confidence as they did on the sunshine and the rain.

J.M. Dunn at his desk at Bangor shed prior to his retirement in September 1958. His Bassett Lowke 'George V' class 4-4-0 is proudly displayed. *Mark Radley*

Max enjoyed a retirement just in excess of 10 years and these were probably the happiest years of his life. He wrote the first of two books - *Reflections on a Railway Career* published by Ian Allan in 1966; he was working on a second publication - 'Further Reflections...' which, whilst finished in draft form, was never published. He catalogued all the photographic negatives taken over a 45-year-long railway career. These, after many years in the 'collectors' wilderness', found their way into the safe archives of the LNWR Society which purchased the collection in 1995 for a figure that would have been beyond Max's wildest dreams and so are available for enthusiasts interested in the areas and period of his career. He wrote at least three books prior to his retirement whilst at Bangor - *The Chester & Holyhead Railway*, *The Wrexham, Mold & Connah's Quay Railway* and *The Stratford upon Avon & Midland Junction Railway* all published by Oakwood Press. To these were added numerous articles in the likes of the *Railway Magazine* plus various dissertations to railway enthusiasts clubs and those interested in railway history. Back in 1962 he became a founder member of the precursor to the present LNWR Society, 'The London & North Western Railway Historical Society'.

On retirement he and Sally had moved south to Robertsbridge, East Sussex, where for a few years they lived in a relatively secluded farmhouse. Their final resting place was a substantial family-owned detached house in Walberton, West Sussex called 'Kennelcroft'. My father and I paid them a visit in the autumn of 1962, the weather was exceedingly wet and we journeyed from Horsley to Barnham Junction via Havant. Some years later I visited alone: it was the August bank holiday weekend of 1966 and for reasons that I will explain later I had not been able to take any form of holiday that summer, so Max very kindly offered to have me over for a long weekend. Having left direct from work on the Friday evening I journeyed from Chester to Crewe and on to Euston, and then from Victoria 'Brighton side' to Barnham Junction. I noted that the last of the London commuters alighted as far away as Arundel! Max was waiting for me on the platform and, pleasantries exchanged, led the way to a pre-booked taxi, a splendid Armstrong Siddeley 'Sapphire' which glided us away to nearby Walberton.

That weekend was one of the most memorable of my mis-spent youth, I think we did little else but talk about railways when we weren't out and about! He had recently finished 'Reflections' which was at the publishers or printers. We joked that the 'Reflections' were akin to those seen in ditchwater - such was his disregard for the final years of his career spent warring with the 'powers that be' from his office in Bangor. My mother always felt that he 'cut off his nose to spite his face' by retiring early thus compromising his full railway pension rights (as a staff member for many years he would have contributed to the superannuation scheme) - but I believe he did the right thing, although he later admitted that royalties from his book amounted to little more than a pittance! By a fortunate coincidence my father's friend Joe Shervington had retired earlier that year and moved from Derbyshire down to nearby Chichester. Joe had sensibly retired at 60 and taken up 'messing about with boats' as a hobby, hence his move (with his wife Alice's full support) to a place near to, but not too near, the sea. That balmy Saturday afternoon we spent sailing his dinghy which he moored at nearby Dell Quay. Sunday morning was spent discussing various branch lines in North Wales with which I was familiar, along with comparisons between LMS engines and their earlier LNWR counterparts and their performances when working said branch lines! (It should be said here that both my dad and occasionally myself were dispatched by Max to map out or photograph the remains of some of the more esoteric railways near our home in Broughton.) The afternoon was a delight, Max, Sally and I set off by bus to the nearby village of Slindon on the South Downs. Here we took a footpath that led to a forested area known as Eartham Wood where we found ourselves walking along Stane Street, the Roman road from London to Chichester. Over 40 years later I can still picture the solid remains of the road running in a straight line over the downs and through those still woods in the direction of Chichester. Max remarked that if perchance we visited on a quiet night when there was a full moon, we might hear the sounds of chariot wheels rumbling over the cobbles! He was always very much a romantic when it came to things 'no longer with us' and when his ideas were queried he would oft recite, 'There are more things in heaven and earth than are dreamt of in man's philosophy!'

One of the endearing things that I recall about Maxwell Dunn was his excitement when he cracked a joke or related a funny story (of which he had many). Even before he got to the punch line or end of the tale he would start to hiss'ss'ss and his false teeth would start to rattle and clack! Two favourites which typically involved the triumph of old over new concerned the old fat lady who got jammed with her shopping on the escalator at Baker Street underground station, everyone; piled up behind her and fell about in total disarray! The other, which Sally loved to relate, was of a very sluggish horse and cart that ventured onto Telford's Menai suspension bridge causing a huge build up of traffic in its rear. Both instances were of course witnessed by their storytellers. If Max had one regret it was that he had never 'made any money' - he went to great pains to instill in me that the most important thing that I should do when I achieved my independence and started to earn properly was to 'accumulate around £20,000 and keep it in the bank!' That way he reckoned people 'would do my bidding and not the other way around!' Well in the mid-1960s twenty grand was a King's ransom, just how he thought a time-served engineer was going to accumulate that amount in a few short years was beyond me then and even today takes a sustained effort of the imagination! He records that when he retired in 1958 his salary was just £763 per annum, even some of his senior drivers were earning almost the same amount!

It says much of him that neither he nor Sally would accept any payment towards my expenses for that memorable weekend and so remembering that Sally liked 'Peters' dark chocolate I went out and bought a number of large bars for her whilst in Bognor Regis on the Monday morning prior to my leaving. Max bade me farewell from the platform at Barnham Junction soon after lunchtime on that bank holiday Monday. We corresponded regularly mainly about railways and he was keen on following the progress of my apprenticeship. Then sadly one evening in March 1969 we received a phone call from Joe Shervington announcing that whilst shaving that morning Max had collapsed and died, seemingly of a heart attack.

Max was interred in nearby Yapton churchyard and whilst I recall seeing his grave in the summer of 1969, I completely failed to locate it when I paid a return visit some 30-odd years later. Sally, who apparently had been suffering from dementia prior to his death, did not recognize me when Joe and I called on her later that summer. She herself passed away soon afterwards in a care home.

Joseph Arthur Reginald Shervington MCIT 1904-1993

Mention has been made previously of one of my father's other life-long friends - Joe Shervington. Unlike Max, my father befriended Joe at school, Harrow County School (or Harrow Grammar as it was later to become known). Joe, who hailed from a large Roman Catholic family (10 children) in Wembley, started his apprenticeship at the Willesden LNWR sheds the year after my father in 1920. His apprenticeship was unindentured and thus at the behest of his father he left after 2½ years to join Messrs Staplefords, a carriage and wagon builder in Coalville, Leicestershire. Having learnt the trade of wagon builder, allied to design engineering experiences gained in the drawing office, he moved on completion of his 'dual apprenticeship' to coal factors Stephenson & Clarke who in the days of private ownership had one of the biggest fleet of coal wagons on the country. Here he worked in the wagon and traffic department as a traffic supervisor looking after the 'speedy & efficient' running and repair of the company's wagons. He was responsible for maintaining supplies of empties at the collieries and docks, etc. and arranging trainload workings with the railway companies as and when possible. During this period Joe became very familiar with all of the country's main railway companies' marshalling yards, docks and coal handling facilities where appropriate to the activities of his employer. In due course he was promoted to the position of chief traffic supervisor. A period of war service followed when, in 1943, he was commissioned into the Royal Engineers-Movement Control Section. I recall him telling me about the period when he had an office on Crewe station from where he supervised troop train movements through the Crewe district. On cessation of the hostilities he rejoined Stephenson Clarke's in his previous position until, in 1947, he joined the newly nationalized National Coal Board as Divisional Transport Officer of the Midlands division based at Chesterfield.

I have fond memories of fairly regular visits from Joe and his wife Alice when they lived in Chesterfield. He was a somewhat larger than life character with a great sense of humour that went with his booming voice and large frame. We were discussing the sort of naughty tricks that schoolboys got up to in our respective youths. I regaled him with tales of placing pennies on the line held down with sticky Fyffe's banana labels and turning them into large thin discs under the wheels of a passing train! He replied with, 'Oh yes we did that too, but best of all we used to hide in the grass outside Harrow-on-the-Hill [GCR] station and when the home signal was pulled off, we would hang on to the wire so that when the signalman released it, it failed to return to danger!' They would then wait for the hapless signalman to descend from his box and walk the 50 yards or so to look at the signal then quietly release the wire returning the signal to danger! Then they would scarper off through the long grass.

He once related to me a tale concerning a visit, by a group of members of one of the better-known railway enthusiast societies, to the colliery* near Chesterfield where he had his office. He had received a written request from the club Secretary for a visit by a specified number of members to look around the surface areas of the said establishment. He readily agreed to the visit which was to take place early one summer evening and, thinking that it might prove of great interest to the visitors, carefully prepared some handout sheets detailing

---

* The colliery was accessed from one side by sidings off the ex-Midland Railway and from the other by sidings off the ex-Great Central main line.

a brief history of the colliery and its output figures etc., etc. When the said 'posse' of enthusiasts had arrived and been herded to his office for a brief talk and the handout of the carefully prepared information, Joe proceeded with a conducted tour of the site. Much to his consternation they paid little or no attention to his efforts and went off to take photographs of the sidings with special attention being paid to an old Midland Railway signal that was sited in the yard! When he finally bade them farewell from his office later in the evening he was somewhat disappointed to find that most of his carefully prepared colliery data sheets had been left behind on the office table. He admitted to me, 'Well, they were a bunch of railway enthusiasts so I suppose I should have known better!'

This reaction from him reminded me that unlike both my father and Max, Joe was not one to wax lyrical about the past but conversely he embraced the modern world of transport and indeed made a very significant contribution to it. He was one of the progenitors, if not the originator, of the 'Merry Go Round' (MGR) coal trains that became universal in shifting bulk trainloads of coal from the pitheads to the power stations, discharging and returning to the pitheads again as the same train, from the late 1960s onwards. I dread to think what he would make of today's fetish for importing the 'black diamonds' from anywhere but the UK. What he did wax lyrical about was the power and efficiency of modern transport over the days of steam. In his later years he frequently visited a hostelry north of Oxford sited beside the ex-GWR main line. There he would sit in the pub garden with a friend supping the local brew watching his beloved 'MGR' coal trains passing by heading for Didcot power station. Referring to the acceleration he once said to me, 'You can fairly admire the way these modern diesel-electrics just get hold of their train!' Well you can't argue with that even if the locomotives at that time (early 1980s) must have been the class '56' Co-Co types and their contemporaries.

Joe was a great 'name dropper' and boasted of sharing a carriage compartment with George Bernard Shaw on an up Great Central train before alighting at Harrow. On another much later occasion he shared a compartment with the TV personality Katie Boyle and listed among his friends well-known people such as Dick Ezra of NCB fame. When he moved to Oxford, he met up with the ex-boss of the Eastern Region Gerry Fiennes* at Paddington station's café once a month for a chat.

As mentioned previously Joe retired to Chichester in 1965 where for a few years he enjoyed sailing his small dinghy and his other hobby of woodworking, before moving with his wife Alice to a bungalow at Bognor Regis in the early 1970s. Alice was a charming lady who became a lasting friend of my parents since meeting them back in the 1930s. Her parents hailed from Vitebsk in Russia and fled to London in 1907 as a result of the anti-Jewish pogroms following the defeat of Russia by the Japanese in 1905. On a humorous note, back in the summer of 1963, following an enjoyable afternoon out in North Wales together,

---

*   Gerry Fiennes was the one time General Manager of the Eastern Region based at Liverpool Street station, London and is well known amongst enthusiasts as the author of a book entitled *I Tried to Run a Railway*.

my mother suggested on arrival back at our home in Broughton that as it was getting late and we had a comfortable spare room, they stay the night before setting off back to Chesterfield the following Sunday. Joe being the driver readily accepted, but Alice was a shade reticent! We found out after they left the following morning that they hadn't slept in the same room for many years on account of Joe's sonorous snoring! Alice regretfully passed away while on holiday in the Isle of Arran in 1976. Joe moved later to a ground floor flat in Oxford where I had the pleasure of visiting him on several occasions. He, being the last survivor of my father's friends, would regale me with amusing tales of their youth and times together. He sadly passed away whilst residing at a nursing home near to his daughter Marya's home in Cumnor in 1993 at the age of 89. Gone but most certainly not forgotten!

Joe Shervington with the author's mother and her granddaughter Gemma at Curzon Park in July 1983.   *Author*

A Llandudno Junction-allocated Midland Compound 4-4-0 has its work cut out on Saturday 17th August, 1957 as it hauls a 10-coach train, probably a Llandudno-Manchester special. Compounds were pressed into heavier services in the summer months both pre- and post-World War II. In his time at Llandudno Junction dad would have been involved in inspections and 'X' repairs on the shed's Compounds. The photograph is taken at Godscroft Lane, between Chester and Warrington. Godscroft Lane signal box is on the left and Helsby Hill dominates in the background.   *Norman Jones*

Ex-GWR Mogul No. 6380 stands at platform 2 at Chester station with a stopping train for Barmouth on 29th May, 1959. BR Standard class '4' 2-6-4T No. 80092 stands ready for duty on the centre road. Note the '57XX' class 0-6-0PT in the Mold bay platform.   *R.S. Carpenter Photos*

Chapter Eleven

Mold Junction, The Final Years

Life at 6B became more and more hectic in the late 1950s but nothing was to prepare the shed staff for the onslaught that was to come early in 1960. A couple of years previously the GWR shed at Chester had been reassigned from the Western Region of BR to the London Midland Region; this was unfortunately the precursor to its closure in April 1960 and subsequent conversion to a major diesel servicing depot for North Wales. The responsibility for servicing and 'turning around' the many ex-GWR engines that came to Chester then became the responsibility of both Chester (LMR) and Mold Junction sheds, the latter handling the bulk of the return Salop-bound freight work. Chester shed being predominantly a 'passenger' shed handled the much lower volume of that traffic. Pressure was exerted on my father to take an allocation of Chester's ex-GWR motive power. This was not well received by him as he saw at first hand the parlous state that a lot of the freight locomotives had been allowed to get into. Also at a time when 6B's allocation of ex-LMS engines was nearing 50 locomotives it made the whole matter untenable. So after much resistance the 'powers that be' conceded to my dad's reasoning and the culprits were sent off down the Western Region to various other freight sheds, Oxley being one of the main recipients. His reward for taking on this extra burden was elevation to the status of a 'Special B' shed master, one step down from the divisional motive power superintendent that carried a pay rise and upgraded the family travel status to first class passes (six per annum).

Now to a young 'whippersnapper' like me it was great news that GWR engines could be found on 'our shed'. The first Sunday morning that I visited after they arrived I distinctly recall 'crowning' myself on the tender brake handle of a '28XX' 2-8-0! You don't forget things like that in a hurry and it taught me to always look up when climbing aboard a GWR tender engine. For a period of about three years the place was a veritable 'spotter's paradise', with locomotives as diverse as Moguls and 'Castles' to be found on shed on a Sunday morning when most of my visits were made. 'Kings' were never seen at Chester due to the roof restriction in Balderton tunnel. (This of course was rectified in preservation days when *King George V* made many visits from its base in Hereford.) Problems became endless: one of the recurring nightmares was the use of hard Yorkshire coal in long GWR fireboxes designed to burn soft, long flame South Wales coal. If former Great Western engines were allowed to leave the shed without having had their grates and ashpans properly cleaned it was a recipe for disaster, one of the main protagonists being the '43XX' Moguls that had a relatively short and narrow firebox. The Mold Junction coal inevitably formed a hard clinker with the remnants of the South Wales ash resulting in a 'green fire', this of course would make itself known on that first hurdle out of Saltney Yard, namely the dreaded Gresford Bank! The number of times my dad came home from work cursing, 'One of those blasted little Great Western 2-6-0s has stopped the place up again!' no doubt with the unforgiving tones of Control

A Stanier 'Black Five' class 4-6-0 heads a Mold Junction-Basford Hall van train (turn No. 121) as it passes Chester No. 1 signal box.   *Bill Price*

Stanier '8F' class 2-8-0 No. 48771 with turn 107 - Mold Junction to Menai Bridge/Holyhead - runs on the down slow line through Prestatyn on 16th May, 1964.   *John Hobbs*

still ringing in his ears. I have fairly reliable tales of 6B fire droppers actually getting pricker bars jammed between the ash pan and the cab roof in desperate efforts to break up the clinker after being reprimanded by Mr Robinson following such catastrophes.

This problem didn't originate at Mold Junction as it was generally deemed that the engines were coming on shed in a parlous state having set out from sheds such as Oxley and Pontypool Road. So one Saturday morning in March 1963, there arose the opportunity to meet up with one of these 2-6-0 culprits at Coton Hill, Shrewsbury. The engine had worked up on a class 'C' freight from Pontypool Road that morning, so my dad hitched a lift on a Salop '5X' 'Jubilee' that was rostered out of Saltney yard that morning, having shedded overnight at 6B. They arrived at Coton Hill just in time to see the crews changing over after the Mogul train's arrival in the down sidings. The young fireman was ex-Chester West (84K) so he obviously knew the problems, and as they had a layover of about an hour before setting off, he quietly started to 'prick out' almost the entire contents of the firebox! That done with a minimum of the old fire remaining he then started to build a new fire carefully (and expertly) placing the coal all around the sides and back of the box. By the time they got the 'right away' the engine was blowing off and continued to do so all the way up the bank through Baschurch! The scariest moment was approaching Cefn viaduct near Ruabon, when my dad recalled that, 'we were going so fast we were pitching and rolling all over the place I thought we'd be going over the side!' I suspect having an ex-LMS shedmaster on board somewhat influenced the ex-GWR men's approach to things, but that engine ran like a dream all the way back to Saltney. So proving that it wasn't the 'song' but the way you 'sang it'. Some time afterwards I asked him what he thought of the '5X' 'Jubilee', his answer came in two words - 'miners' friend'!

Many were the times that he came home from work with woe begotten tales of the chronic conditions of GWR engines. One day a fire dropper knocked on his office door and begged him to take a look at what he had found in the smokebox of a '28XX' 2-8-0. Opening the smokebox door had revealed a mass of bitumen, some burnt, some not, that had settled around the blastpipe neck solidifying into an immovable lump. Clearly the engine had been left in steam in an old pitch-roofed shed with the heat issuing from the chimney busy working away at the tar that sealed the edifice from the elements! On another occasion one of the fitters asked him to look at a main frame fissure on a '28XX' that some individual had previously tried to repair by bolting two fishplates either side of it! Problems notwithstanding, he did have a healthy respect for the designs of Churchward and Collett. During a visit to the shed in the summer of 1963, whilst in my father's office our conversation was interrupted by a panicking shed turner* who had found what he believed to be a serious leak on one of the injectors beneath the cab of a 'Grange' that was due to go 'off shed'. Led by the turner my dad and I rushed down to the engine in question (No. 6833 *Calcot Grange*), by now halted by its crew on the scissors crossover by the running shift foreman's (RSF) office. Seizing the opportunity to take advantage of the agile teenager that happened to be present, my dad asked me to get down

---

* Shed turner - a driver no longer allowed to work on the main line who was responsible for arranging locomotives to be in the right positional order and facing the right direction for their next turn of duty. He also looked after engine servicing and movements in the general shed area.

Chester West's immaculate 'Castle' class 4-6-0 No. 5033 *Broughton Castle* crosses the Dee bridge at Chester on 28th October, 1958 with a Birkenhead-Bournemouth through train. Note the horsebox, this would not be a popular addition to the train from the footplate crew's point of view as it would enforce 60 mph running, 'Castles' would frequently exceed 90 mph on the flat approaches to Shrewsbury. A colour photograph might have revealed an interesting hue of blood & custard Gresley, green Bulleid and brown & cream Mk I stock! The engine would probably have worked as far as Oxford. A Bournemouth crew and locomotive (probably a Bulleid Pacific) would work forward from there.   *S.D. Wainwright*

Right: With the United Colliery home signal giving a clear road ahead, near the top of Gresford bank, ex-Chester West driver Ernie Ellis (by this time a Mold Junction man) hammers 'Modified Hall' class 4-6-0 No. 7925 *Westol Hall* of Cardiff (Canton) south when in charge of the 'Cardiff Lights'. This was a 'C' or 'D' class fitted freight train. This photograph evokes memories of that superbly sharp Great Western exhaust bark.   *Cleve Jones*

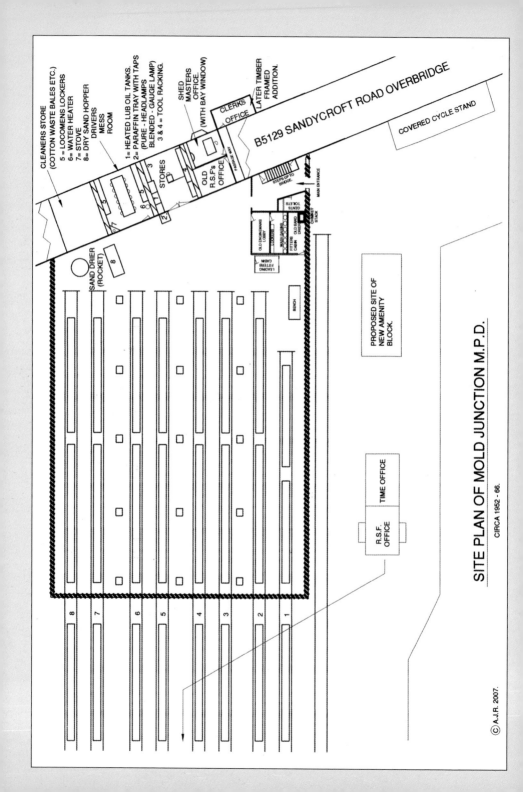

SITE PLAN OF MOLD JUNCTION M.P.D.

CIRCA 1952 - 66.

© A.J.R. 2007.

on all-fours and look under the cab to see where the leak was coming from. I quickly ascertained that it was being caused by a split in the injector overflow pipe and therefore not at all serious, and so the engine was allowed to leave. The favoured locomotives were indeed the '68XX' 'Granges' that would 'steam on a pack of firelighters', and perhaps his favourite locomotive was the express freight '47XX' 2-8-0 that was 'Churchward's masterpiece'. Not that we saw many at Mold Junction, Birkenhead being the more regular destination for these machines.

He regarded the four-cylinder 'Castles' as a 'Rolls Royce amongst locomotives' such was the finesse of the engineering. Many ex-LMS drivers might disagree considering that on an engine not blessed with a mechanical lubricator (as most weren't) there were about 97 oiling points to take care of prior to leaving the shed! His biggest gripes were the tube size which being of relatively small bore compared to ex-LNWR or LMS engines was the main cause of problems for the shed staff; along with the clinkering and somewhat 'old fashioned' Swindon grate cleaning method necessary, i.e. no rocker grates. When 'fire dropping' the procedure was (via the fire hole door) to dig out what was left of the burning clinker and throw it off the footplate into skips alongside the ash pit. Your author didn't realize this and once when walking alongside a GWR locomotive at the ash pit was almost incinerated by a shovel load of red hot ash that came sailing off the footplate landing in the narrow gauge 'tub' beside where he was walking!

My father took great pride in his home-allocated locomotives and it was generally deemed that a 6B engine was a good 'un'. This, of course, brought problems as when times were busy these 'good 'uns' tended to go missing, commandeered by other sheds to stand in for their own 'lame ducks'! It also became known at Western Region sheds that 6B was a good place to send 'lame ducks', as usually they would receive corrective attention and arrive back at their home sheds in far better condition than when they set out. Fortunately, my dad soon cottoned on to this malpractice and began dispatching these culprits back whence they came. Both he and his deputies took great delight in hassling Control until a path could be found to get them away from Mold Junction. I recall that we were once journeying north from Euston when upon reaching Bletchley he spotted one of his class '5s' standing in a siding near the station. The air in the compartment quickly turned a pale shade of blue, 'That b … y engine's been missing for weeks - just wait till I get hold of Control …!'

The year 1960 was quite a notable one as the shed was not just graced by the influx of Great Western locomotives but also a small contingent of 'Green Namers' from the home Region in the form of four 'Baby Scots' that came south from Carnforth shed. Not particularly popular with the 6B footplate men, they thankfully they didn't stay long as with their January arrival came departures exactly three months later just as the GWR engines started to descend on the overstretched shed.

As the shed had been elevated in importance in the general scheme of things, my father saw fit to petition the 'powers that be' for much needed improved shed amenities. Apart from the 'new' RSF's and time office that had been built post-war in between the shed's No. 4 and 5 roads out on the 'shed bank', the

BR Standard '9F' class 2-10-0 No. 92018 at Mold Junction shed *circa* 1960. In the background are the running shift foreman's office, the time office, and the old coaling stage and water tank.

Geoff Kent

All 'shined up and away to go' with the 'Jones Balers' special is driver Maurice (Moy) Williams with his 6B steed, Stanier 'Black Five' 4-6-0 No. 45001. The train pulls out of the company's sidings at Mold, this was a fitted class 'C' special that was an export train to the Continent via Harwich. To my recollection 6B worked the train as far ar Basford Hall sidings, Crewe.

C. Jones Collection

internal facilities had by the early 1960s become grim to say the least. Certainly the LMS 'modernization' programme had ensured that the old LNWR northlight roof had been removed and replaced with the then standard longitudinal concrete smoke vent and glazing design, albeit at the expense of the shed's overall length. This was cut back at the time of re-roofing so that only a Stanier class '5' and a '3F' 'Humpy' 0-6-0T could be housed together under cover on all but the No. 1 road which was shorter still. This road (furthest from the main line) was generally used to house the breakdown van. A plan was mooted for a staff amenity block to be built adjacent to the sand bunker outside the rear of the shed. This block would house toilets and wash facilities for the drivers/firemen/fitters, etc., plus locker rooms and recreational/mess rooms and kitchen, etc. I recall my father working out suggested layouts for the building on his drawing board at home, nevertheless nothing ever transpired as I believe the idea came too late in the shed's anticipated lifespan to be deemed an economic viability.

Every so often it would be called upon Mold Junction shed to assist in a special duty. Being a mainly freight shed there was little of excitement concerning special passenger workings, save for the occasional need for a back-up engine for a Royal train working, even so such engines (usually a Stanier class '5' 4-6-0) would be polished until the buffers shone. A prime example of this was when, following her coronation in 1953, Queen Elizabeth visited North Wales as part of her and the Duke of Edinburgh's tour of Great Britain. Another occasion that I can remember concerns a special freight working in April 1960. This was an export special for 'Jones Balers' in Mold that was booked to run from the company's sidings in Mold to Harwich and thence over to Holland and Germany.

This train was worked by Mold Junction men and their specially polished steed, 6B class '5' No. 45001, as far as Basford Hall Sidings, Crewe. The occasion even made the local papers, such was the importance of local companies and their products in those halcyon days, especially when a thrust was made to get those products into the European markets!

Some amusing anecdotes

I am indeed indebted to some of the surviving 'lads' from 6B who on hearing of my efforts to put together this book were only too pleased to relate, or for that matter put some more meat on the bones of my own sparse memories of, some of the more interesting and amusing things that happened at the shed in its latter years.

Bill Price of Northop has some amusing stories to tell from when he was a young fireman and later a driver. One in particular involves a southbound freight working from Preston on a winter's evening after dark in the early 1960s. Having been halted near Preston No. 1 box they were warned by the signalman to look out for a 'body on the line' as a down passenger train had just arrived at the station with a carriage door swinging open so it was assumed that somebody had fallen or jumped from the train. Bill was told by his driver to

Mold Junction driver Joe Aldridge (formerly of Chester Northgate CLC) poses on Stanier '8F' class 2-8-0 No. 48655 at Hendre Quarry sidings in 1963. Notice the lowered top lamp bracket, compliant with the recently introduced overhead wire regulations.   *Cleve Jones*

lean over the side of the engine (a 6B Stanier '8F') and using his hand lamp try to locate the cadaver that might be lying in the 'six foot', meanwhile having been permitted to 'enter section under caution' they proceeded south at a snail's pace so as not to miss anything that might show up. Having just passed under the skew bridge south of Leyland Bill spotted something lying by the track. The driver brought the train to a halt, and they both climbed down from the engine. Now as they approached the body, Bill's mate (who shall remain nameless) uttered the words, 'Let's have a look in his wallet first!' To this day Bill doesn't know whether he was joking or not for as they got near to the body it sat up and rubbing its head uttered the words, 'Where am I?' The story ends happily as he was taken aboard the engine and deposited at the next signal box from where an ambulance was summoned.

Another story involves Hendre limeworks on the Mold-Denbigh line. Hendre was a point about mid-way between Rhydymwyn and Nannerch that produced a considerable amount of lime and lead ore traffic for the Chester, Mold and Denbigh branch. Indeed for some years after the line was closed to passenger traffic a truncated section was kept open as far as Dolfechlas crossing signal box where the company's private sidings branched off on the up side of the line. It was from here that the BR loco crews handed over to, or collected their trains from, the lime company's 'shunting tractor', a one time Muir Hill device on four tractor wheels fitted with a shunting 'buffer' beam and towing shackles. There were strict instructions to BR staff not to enter the works sidings with locomotives unless really necessary and as for going beneath the covered loading hopper, this was absolutely forbidden. On one particular trip in the later years the 6B crew (Bill and mate) arrived to pick up the daily lime 'Presflo' wagons and were informed that the precious Muir Hill had broken down and so could not draw out the wagons from beneath the loading hopper. In fact the loaded wagons were parked beyond the hopper at the back end of the siding! Usual motive power for these workings was a Stanier '8F' and so it was agreed they would ease the beast slowly and carefully down the rickety track and under the lime-encrusted hooding until they could couple up. 'Presflos' were modern fitted wagons and so the brakes had to be 'blown off' and the regulator opened as carefully as possible - all to no avail, a snowstorm resulted! When they got back to Mold Junction, having uncoupled their train in the Mold End sidings, they went 'on shed' with their 'White Eight' and were greeted by a chorus of 'We know where you've been!' from the comedians in the shed yard.

Ex-fireman Cleve Jones has an amusing tale of when as a young cleaner fresh out of school his command of the English vocabulary was not all that he might have wished for. One fine day when instructed by my father to add some water softening tablets to the main water tank he wasn't sure about how many to add so being rightly cautious he asked Mr Robinson how many he should add. 'Oh just a couple' came the reply from the boss as he walked off. 'A couple?' thought Cleve who wasn't sure how many a couple was! This time he decided against displaying his ignorance and so took a chance and threw in about a dozen! I dread to think what the direct result of that was (*see Chapter Six on technical matters concerning boiler priming*).

Driver Emrys Williams eases 6B's star balanced Stanier '8F' class 2-8-0 No. 48749 out of Hendre limeworks siding onto what was once the Mold-Denbigh main line, but by 1964 reduced to a single line headshunt. The train consisted of about 24 wagons and would stop at Mold for weighing, at which point the vacuum-fitted 'Presflos' would be marshalled next to the engine to give assisted braking down Kinnerton bank, hence negating the need to stop again at Pen-y-Ffordd to 'pin down'. Somewhat unusually the '8F' sports a welded tender.   *Emrys Williams*

Today the trackbed remains as road access to what is left of the works, now the property of Associated Wire Products. The Olwyn Goch pit head gear once accessing a 463 ft deep shaft leading to the lead ore and lime deposits has long gone, but much of the original works remains. It is interesting to note that the bottom of the shaft connected with a drainage tunnel that ran from the old Pantymwyn lead mine, a couple of miles to the south, right through to Bagillt on the Dee Estuary.   *Author*

Chapter Twelve

Accidents

Regrettably, as most railwaymen will know, their environment is probably one of the most dangerous places to work and even more dangerous for the uninitiated. As recounted in an earlier chapter my father was a member of the St John's Ambulance Brigade and its training had often proved extremely useful when dealing with accidents in and around engine sheds. Most accidents on railways that the public hears of concern those which involve members of the public when entering or trespassing on railway property. There were at least two such occasions when 6B engines and footplate crews were involved in horrific accidents on the North Wales coast main line where children had attempted to cross the line in the Abergele-Rhyl area between caravan camps and been run down. This usually culminated in an inquest that the crew involved and my father had to attend if it was a Mold Junction working. It goes without saying that the trauma greatly affected the locomen, especially if a death resulted.

There were many minor accidents on the shed itself which were treatable with first aid, but there were a couple of very bad accidents where my father was involved. One involved a fire dropper's mate, Joe Larkin, who was working beneath an engine on the ashpit. He had placed an already running hosepipe near to the wheel alongside the engine before going underneath. As he reached out for the hose the engine was accidentally pushed forward by the next locomotive in line and Joe lost his forearm beneath the wheels. The experience did not prevent Joe from returning to work at the shed where he remained as a storeman until closure many years later.

Another far worse event occurred when driver Arthur Hughes mounted the rear of a tender to 'put the bag in'. He slipped and fell to the ground and broke his neck across a buffer. Unsurprisingly, he died of his injuries.

Back in 1964 a young and inexperienced fireman at Llandudno Junction got his head crushed between buffers when coupling up. No doubt such tales would send shivers down the spine of any engineman who did such mundane tasks several times a day, probably without thinking of the dangers.

Most sheds operating within the areas aligned to the electrification of the West Coast main line were equipped with mock overhead line gallows along one of the shed roads. These were so called as they closely resembled old fashioned execution gallows and usually consisted of four or five support poles with a mock 'live' wire strung between them at the exact height from the rail of the actual wires to be found radiating from Crewe on all the main routes excepting the Chester, North Staffs and Shrewsbury lines. There had been several tragic accidents involving footplate staff that just didn't appreciate the dangers of getting themselves or their coal tools near to the live 25KV wires. I recall my father relating a tale of a fireman climbing up on top of a tender and it was only when he looked back and saw that his driver's face was white with fear that he realised the position he was in at that very moment. He virtually fell

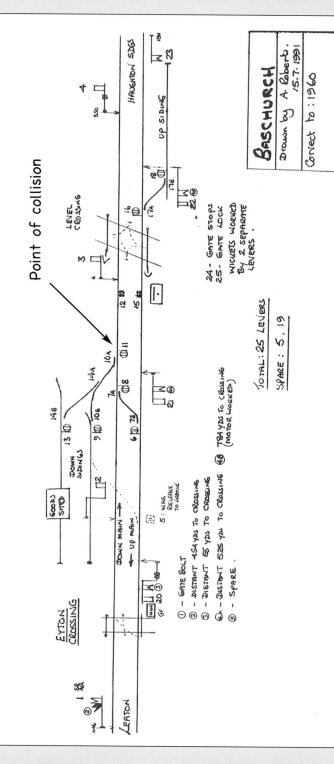

Plan showing the site of the Baschurch accident.

John Dixon

out of that tender to get clear of the lethal wire just inches from him! It was for just these reasons that the mock gallows were erected and all footplate staff had to undergo training with an appointed safety officer on what was permissible practice under the wires and what was not. After the training session each 'student' had to sign an indemnification form releasing his employer from any liability in case of an accident – cold comfort indeed.

Baschurch

Generally there was an excellent record of safety regarding serious accidents, naturally breakdowns were frequent but these rarely involved any kind of personal injury or trauma beyond 'taking the blame' for causing the derailment or whatever. However, there was one particular accident 'caused' by Mold Junction men that resulted in the loss of life of one Swindon- and two Salop-based railwaymen.

It happened on the evening of 13th February, 1961 when the 6B men were working the 6.25 pm unfitted goods train from Coton Hill yard north of Shrewsbury to Saltney just south of Chester. For reasons unknown they were late getting away from Coton Hill and so on reaching Baschurch were halted and requested by the signalman to set back into the down refuge siding. Having stopped in the station they then proceeded to set back in the dark with only a ground signal to confirm that the siding road was clear. An up express passed them on its way south and shortly after this the driver (an ex-Abergavenny LNWR man, Norman Barber from Ewart Street, Saltney Ferry) felt a sudden and hard resistance and naturally thought they had hit the stop block at the end of the siding. The engine and several wagons were at this juncture still out on the main line, so Norman decided as he was unsure of the length of his train and couldn't see any red light indication from the guard, to get off the footplate and walk back down the train to investigate. As he was walking he turned around and saw that the down signal was clear so assumed they had been given the road to Ruabon. He then returned to the footplate where his mate (fireman Brian Dilley also of 6B) was keeping watch, whistled to indicate they were leaving and set off down the main line. Brian then shouted that he could see a glow in the darkness that was behind their train, initially Vic thought it was the receding firebox glow from the up express but quickly realized that it was fast approaching them! With seconds to spare both men jumped off the footplate then there was an horrific crash as the northbound express hit the wagons further back down their train. The engine (ex-GWR 'Hall' class No. 6949 *Haberfield Hall* of 84C Banbury shed) ploughed onto the up tracks and turned onto its side killing the driver and fireman, both of 89A (Shrewsbury) Coleham shed. The first vehicle in the train was a stores van and this plus the leading coach mounted the engine, the van burst into flames killing the occupant, a stores man from Swindon. There was a generally held belief that propane bottles in the stores van were responsible for the rapid and uncontrollable spread of fire that consumed the van. Strangely it was reported in local papers as 'The Silent Train Crash' as even villagers living near the line did not hear the

Recovery work is underway at Baschurch.

collision and were not aware of its occurrence until the fire, plus the arrival of the fire services and their subsequent arc lights, lit up the sky!

At the subsequent inquiry the HM Inspector of Railways, Colonel McMullen, questioned the signalman who (in the darkness) thought that the goods train was safely 'inside' and backed up his claim by stating that he tried the points, which moved without resistance before setting the main line to 'clear'. The inspector who was not happy with this explanation, felt that as far as the signalman was concerned the point blades could easily have been between the wheels of a goods vehicle and therefore free to move! In fact the leading vehicle, a bogie bolster wagon laden with pipes, was astride the point blades when disaster struck. Also there was some doubt as to the actions of the goods guard, C.P. Catterall, who despite believing the train was 'well inside' couldn't remember whether he had screwed down the brake in his van or not - this would seem to give an explanation for the sudden rearwards resistance felt by the driver! Most of the above information has been gleaned from contemporary newspaper reports that omitted to give details of the goods engine but my enquiries with former Mold Junction men reveal that it was an ex-GWR '28XX' class 2-8-0 No. 2856 of 84E Tyseley shed, Birmingham. As the 'Hall' class locomotive involved does not appear in the shed allocation lists after that date, I think it's fair to assume the engine was scrapped as a result of the accident. One positive thing that did emerge was that 6B fireman Brian Dilley received a commendation from the Railway Inspectorate for his prompt and cool-headed action in running forward to the signal box to ensure that both up and down lines were protected from further oncoming traffic.

The Brook Lane Pile-up

This accident happened around the years 1960/61 and was witnessed at first hand by 6B fireman Cleve Jones, unfortunately some of the details have been lost in the mists of memory and time! It happened in the earliest of the days when Mold Junction men began getting involved in the Western Region freight workings to and from the Chester district. Cleve and his mate were inside the Chester No. 5 signal box waiting to relieve a southbound oil train working that was due in from the Stanlow refinery at Ellesmere Port. The train was Shrewsbury bound and from Stanlow to Chester was worked by an ex-GWR 2-6-2T Prairie tank of the '51XX' class. Cleve and his mate, who was sitting in the signal box engrossed in a newspaper, were to work the train forward to Salop with an ex-GWR 'Grange' class 4-6-0 that was standing outside the signal box on the main line. Suddenly the signalman shouted 'she's running away' and ran out of the box as the said oil train came around the corner from under Brook Lane bridge and with the brakes squealing ran into the back of the 'Grange' at about 10 mph!

Pandemonium broke out as the oil tanks piled up against the engines and then tipped over onto their sides and with buffers puncturing the leading tanks, oil gushed out all over the tracks around the signal box. By the grace of God the cargo was lubricating oil and not petroleum otherwise our witness would not be alive to tell the tale, indeed the whole of the Brook Lane bridge and yard area would have been an inferno! The driver of the tank engine was Vic Jones of 89A Coleham shed but his fireman's identity has yet to be ascertained along with that of the 6B driver. It is understood that Vic survived but was highly traumatized and did not go back on the main line as a direct result of the accident.

Chester 6A 'Midland' shed's breakdown gang and crane were quickly on the scene supervised by the DMPS Mr Fairhead. One would surmise that maybe the train, no doubt loose coupled and unfitted, was too heavy for the tank engine which would have lacked the extra braking power of a tender. No doubt there would have been no pinning down of wagon brakes in view of the relatively mild down gradient approaching Chester from Upton. The line has a down gradient from Capenhurst to Mollington so by the time Upton was reached the driver might well have realized that he was in trouble!

A Rude Awakening

In May 1961 my father was admitted into the Royal Infirmary at Chester for a minor operation. It was the first time in his life that he had entered a hospital as an in-patient and he spent about five days (and nights) in the surgical ward which overlooked Chester racecourse (the Roodee) and of course the main line as it emerged from the city walls immediately to the west of the city. At that point the railway is elevated on a long viaduct that runs along the entire northern flank of the Roodee. In those days it carried four tracks with the nearest two carrying the ex-GWR trains to Shrewsbury and beyond, these also doubled up as the up and down slow lines along the North Wales coast as far as Mold Junction No. 1 box. Here the layout involved crossovers to put the slow lines outside of the fast lines which, near the hospital, where the two furthest tracks emerging from the city walls and tunnels etc. The four tracks at that point climbed a short bank out of the city of 1 in 414 before levelling off onto the Roodee viaduct.

Medically the week was a success and a sabbatical for my dad who welcomed the relief from the grinding pressure of work at the shed. He emerged full of praise for the nursing staff who came out 'top of the class' for their quality of care and dedication to the patients in their charge. However, the same cannot be said for his fellow railwaymen as he and the other inmates of the ward had quite an awakening experience each night. From around 1960 the incursion of diesel traction in the form of the English Electric type '4s' (later to become known as the class '40') began to make itself felt on the heavier passenger workings originating from Euston and Holyhead. Naturally the Irish mails were among the first trains to be so hauled and the down night working of this train left Chester at about 12.45 am each morning. As invariably the down fast line was clear at that ungodly hour the crew wasted no time opening up the throttle as they came up the bank out of the Northgate tunnels. Anyone who has any memory of these beasts will know that under full throttle they make an absolutely cachophonous roar! Add that to the audible shock of emerging from a sound muting tunnel at speeds of 40 mph and accelerating and one can imagine the effects on the nearby slumbering patients! Well I think it was the second or third night of my dad's hospitalization that finally did it, one of the patients with whom he had struck up a friendly relationship (a well-known local estate agent) went into a shock induced fit at the sudden awakening caused by the said train. Apparently the man was in a somewhat precarious state after an op that evening and this experience came close to finishing him off! My father was absolutely furious having been awoken on the previous nights by the same 'racket'. I think whilst still in hospital he penned a letter to the 'powers that be' at Crewe explaining just how serious a problem the noise from these locomotives was. He also advised that all engine crews should be reminded of the lineside presence of the hospital by a clearly worded sign as they emerged from the Northgate tunnels.

Well his advice was heeded and strict instructions were issued to keep throttles from being fully opened until well clear of the vicinity and in due course a sign was erected to remind the offenders. So not a bad ending to what could have been a tragic event. It also kicked off a lasting friendship between my father and the estate agent who just happened to share the same surname.

Twenty years later the class '40s' could still be seen working through Chester. This view was taken near Crane Street in the 1970s. *S.D. Wainwright*

Mold Junction *circa* 1964. Various changes took place among the local divisions a year previously, one of which was the relocation of Birkenhead shed from the Chester district (6) to Liverpool Edge Hill district (8). Edwin Owen (running shift foreman) stands in front of a Birkenhead shed's (8H) Hughes/Fowler 'Crab' class 2-6-0 No. 42936. The reporting number suggests that it had come on shed after having worked a special passenger duty.   *E.N. Kneale*

Chapter Thirteen

1964 And All That - 45 Years On

By the beginning of 1963 my mother was becoming restless with life in Broughton and was pressuring my dad for a move to a private residence nearer to Chester. She had become acutely aware that not buying a house back in the 1940s had been a profound mistake. As my father's retirement was less than five years away she rightly wanted a move whilst he was still working and therefore able to afford it. By now, due to the closure of the Mold & Denbigh branch to passenger services, he had to make the journey all the way to Mold Junction on this trusty moped (in all weathers!); not that this bothered him but it bothered my mum. So after exploring various properties in and around Chester an address in the somewhat 'up market' area known as Curzon Park was decided on and so in December 1963 we moved to an unassuming 1920s built semi in Park Road West. As I was within two years of taking my GCE examinations the local Flintshire education authorities allowed me to continue my education at Hawarden. To get there each morning it was required that I walk the short distance down to Saltney (just over the Welsh border) from where I was able to catch the school bus. For my father the journey to the shed was just over a mile and so not troublesome in the least.

My daily promenade was most interesting as I passed by Saltney Junction, always the scene of some activity with ex-GWR engines coming away from Saltney yard light after having deposited their night freights from South Wales or wherever, and usually a North Wales-bound passenger working to be observed. Saltney yard was only a short distance from our new abode and if one suffered from insomnia the muted sounds of shunting activities could be heard going on for most of the night, the only time the yard closed was on Sundays.

I have many memories of contented hours spent watching the goings-on at the yard but unhappily I never took a camera - couldn't afford the film! I had long before developed a special fondness for things Great Western. Somehow from the (generally clean) liveries of locomotives and coaches along with lineside bric-à-brac, chocolate and cream signal boxes and signals with finials etc., the Western Region had managed to retain its pre-nationalization identity whereas the London Midland Region seemed to have just disappeared into the morass of the post-war monolithic organization. As a child this interest was deemed somewhat 'unpatriotic' by my dad and when my Aunt Sophie presented me with a Hornby-Dublo *Cardiff Castle* for Christmas back in 1960, he followed up a year later with the Stanier 2-8-0 which at that time was considered a very convincing model!

Prior to moving from Broughton I took many a cycle ride with my pals out to a place called Balderton some three miles to the east where the ex-GWR main line crossed the Chester to Kinnerton road. Here we would not have to wait long at the crossing gates before there would come those familiar 'ding dings' from the adjacent signal box signifying an imminent train that, if an express passenger, would hurtle through at 60-plus - happy days! From those sightings

Fire and water! An ash fire in a wagon is swiftly dealt with by one-armed Albert (Mark Sabre) Sproston, always eager to get a break from the monotony of Mold Junction's time office! The coaling plant is to the right.

E.N. Kneale

at that spot I can remember seeing the following named engines: Nos. 7019 *Fowey Castle*, 1024 *County of Pembroke*, 1016 *County of Hants* (also 'cabbed' in Chester station), 5942 *Doldowlod Hall*, 6958 *Oxburgh Hall*, 6994 *Baggrave Hall*, 7907 *Hart Hall* and many more) now forgotten as I never went out with the aim of trainspotting with a note book. The cleaner an engine was the more likely the sighting would stay in the memory.

At some point in early 1964 my father was faced with a dilemma, the resulting decision that he made got him into some trouble with the 'powers that be'. A seriously 'lame' 'Hall' class locomotive had arrived on shed requiring urgent attention to its driving axle horn blocks. Repair facilities at the ex-Cambrian Railways Oswestry works had been withdrawn and with no nearer availability of a wheel drop he elected to send the engine off down to Llandudno Junction for attention on their wheel drop. As they had been attending to other classes of ex-GWR engines since the LMR takeover of the northern lines, he saw no problem in this course of action. The engine was sent 'light' via the down slow line as pathing permitted; however, when running through the old low and non-recessed (un-modernized) Chester & Holyhead Railway platforms at Bagillt and Mostyn the GWR cylinder covers clouted the sides of the said structures and the locomotive arrived at its destination in a somewhat sorry external condition! If he had done his homework (or even consulted his by now retired pal Max Dunn) he would have discovered that back in May 1954 No. 6971 *Athelhampton Hall* had worked a special from West Bromwich through to Llandudno without an engine change at Chester! This engine had scraped several platforms and as a result was impounded at Llandudno Junction pending its return as an 'OGLO' (telegraphic parlance for 'out of gauge load').

The move to Curzon Park had brought our abode nearer to the shed and as we now had a house with a garage there was so much more room to house the moped along with my push bike etc. Even a greenhouse, so my dad could indulge his long held ambition to successfully grow tomatoes. His colleagues at 6B were forever ribbing him about being too 'posh' to associate with them any more! Even my school pals were giving me similar treatment, it seemed that we had the best of all worlds with the grand old city of Chester within walking distance. Easter 1964 found me down at Llandudno Junction once more having a short break at my grandmother's house. I was preparing to return home a couple of days after Easter and strangely my mother's brother Norman called in out of the blue (no phone there in those days). He seemed agitated and wanted to make sure that I was indeed going home that afternoon. No problem there, I was almost ready to leave for my train back to Chester when he called and I soon bade my farewells accordingly. When I got home later that afternoon I was greeted by my mother who was somewhat distressed, she led me upstairs to their bedroom where my dad was lying half asleep. His face was badly bruised with his head bandaged. She then reported that he had only just been returned from hospital and was quite heavily drugged. He had had an accident on his moped that morning on the way to the shed. Apparently when he got as far as Park Avenue in Saltney a bus had pulled out in front of him and started to accelerate away with him close behind it. The bus driver had spotted a late

May 1964 and my dad receives his clock marking 45 years unbroken railway service from Mr Walker Smith - the district motive power superintendent. Mr Thatcher, his assistant, is to the right, the gent on the left is as yet unidentified. At the time of his presentation dad was actually off work recovering from his motorcycle accident, as his blackened right eye testifies! The location I believe was the then recently erected area head office sited on the former trackbed of the old wagon repair shops near Chester General station. *Author's Collection*

The plate adorning the clock presented to my dad. *Author*

BRITISH RAILWAYS
J. E. ROBINSON
IN APPRECIATION OF 45 YEARS' SERVICE

passenger running behind and slammed on his brakes unexpectedly, the resulting collision sent my father clean through the rear window of the bus and he wound up unconscious on the floor of the lower passenger deck! Sadly he had nothing but his trilby hat to protect his head and face, something we just can't countenance today but in those days it was very unusual to see someone wearing a crash helmet when riding a moped.

Despite smashing the rear window of the bus it seemed that he had only suffered mild concussion with some cuts and bruises. He was therefore allowed home on the strict understanding that he spend a couple of days in bed and report to his local GP, a tall imposing middle-aged man by the name of Dr Fricker who lived in nearby in Carrick Road. Dr Fricker subsequently signed him off work and so he spent some weeks convalescing in the peaceful surroundings of his new home. It was during this period that he was visited by Mr Thatcher, assistant to the new DMPS for the Chester district - Mr Walker Smith. His visit was two-fold, firstly to ascertain my father's state of health and secondly to advise him that if he was fit enough they would like him to attend the presentation of the mantelpiece clock to mark 45 years of uninterrupted service to the railway. Well you may recall from Chapter One that he started his apprenticeship at Willesden shed in May 1919, it was now May 1964. Wild horses wouldn't have kept him away!

Whilst he was convalescing I inspected the moped that had been stored at Saltney police station. I was shocked to see how badly the front telescopic forks had been bent, effectively the machine was beyond economic repair and we gave it to a relative who tried unsuccessfully to effect a repair - so good riddance to something that became an anathema to our memories. Before May was out he had recovered sufficiently well and would soon be returning to work, and it has to be said that up until that point he made daily calls to the running shift foreman and/or his deputies to ensure that all was well in his kingdom! Sometime during June 1964 he returned to work and just got on with a job that was getting more and more difficult as each month passed by.

A general view of Mold Junction shed on 4th October, 1964.   *R.S. Carpenter Photos*

'Royal Scot' class 4-6-0 No. 46115 *Scots Guardsman* eases in reverse across the scissors at Mold Junction having had clearance from No. 2 signal box to go off shed. The locomotive is in grimy condition, the nameplate has been removed and the speedometer cable disconnected from its crank. The ugly yellow stripe on the cabside indicates its ban on working south of Crewe. I seem to recall my dad saying that the real reason for the ban was the overhead wire clearance in Kilsby & Crick tunnel south of Rugby.

E.N. Kneale

For some weeks during the summer of 1964 an ex-GWR engine had come to the rescue of the East End shunt at Mold Junction. The shed had had their allocation of three Fowler 0-6-0T 'Humpys' reduced to two and both were 'sick' and the yards were now worked by three 350 hp diesel shunters. One of these grumbling beasts had succumbed to a not uncommon serious illness and had been withdrawn to Chester diesel depot for repairs, and so Croes Newydd came to the rescue with one of their trusty pannier tanks. According to my father it did a fine job, outclassing the 'Humpys' and was certainly no worse than the 350s!

By 1963 the northern reaches of the old GWR i.e. from Banbury and Craven Arms northwards had been assigned over to the London Midland Region. Sadly from that point on the old identity started to fade, the most modern and short-lived being the loss of the 'Warship' and 'Western' class diesel-hydraulics which had started to appear on the Paddington-Birkenhead expresses such as the 'Zulu' and 'Birkenhead Flyer'. These were quickly replaced north of Wolverhampton by the (soon to be ubiquitous) Brush type '4s'. I remember my first sighting of a 'Hall' shorn of name and number plates arriving at Mold Junction, this from the bay window of my dad's office in July 1963. This was a precursor of things to come for by the end of 1964 there were very few nameplates adorning any locomotive, whether ex-GWR or LMS.

By the summer of 1965 my father reported that there was only about one ex-GWR engine per day coming onto the shed and by then Chester and Shrewsbury (Coleham) sheds were working the majority of the passenger diagrams with Stanier (go anywhere) class '5s'. The very last personal sighting that I can recall of an ex-GWR engine working a passenger train was of a very grimy No. 6831 *Bearley Grange* heading through Saltney Junction with a Paddington-bound train in November 1965. I also remember, that month, my dad showing me the BR directive that from 31st December, 1965 all remaining Swindon-built GWR-designed locomotives were to be withdrawn from traffic and placed in storage pending disposal (i.e. scrapping)! Strangely the ex-GWR local shed Wrexham Croes Newydd hung on to their trusty '57XX' panniers like grim death, these could be seen working the branches around their home shed i.e. Brymbo and Minerva well into 1966. Indeed I witnessed two of them running coupled up the Manchester line from Chester through Guilden Sutton in July of that year, probably to access the CLC line at Mickle Trafford Junction where they would reverse back to Dee Marsh Junction on the old GCR line, no doubt to work a train back up to Wrexham. I think this says a lot for their reputation as one of the best 0-6-0 tank engines ever designed, as their capability and reliability was supreme.

If things had become depressing on the ex-GWR scene around Chester by late 1965, then it should be remembered that the situation with ex-LMS engines was not much better. The railway hierarchy had become obsessed with modernization to the utter detriment of the steam sheds that still remained in operation. Dr Beeching had made it quite clear that the steam engine was to be got rid of as quickly as possible and this attitude had cascaded down to everyone concerned, despite the fact that most of the revenue earning traffic was freight, and that was still mainly hauled by steam locomotives. All steam enthusiasts of my generation will remember the parlous state that engines were

Cleve Jones had his photograph taken against his 'nearly namesake', 'Grange' class 4-6-0 No. 6850 *Cleeve Grange* outside Mold Junction shed. Whilst the locomotive retains her nameplates and numberplates, the smokebox door number and shedplate have been removed.   *Ernie Ellis*

Mold Junction yard *circa* 1965. An excellent view in bright sunshine of my dad's right-hand man, the leading running shift foreman Tom (Pensarn) Jones standing by one of 6B's well maintained STanier 'Black Five' class 4-6-0s, No. 45325. Tom was so called because he hailed from Llandudno Junction where as a boy he attended Pensarn school (along with my mother).   *E.N. Kneale*

allowed to get into in those final years; not that this was the fault of shed staff who were overworked and undermanned as more and more people left the railway disillusioned at what a once proud operation had by then become. I think it was in November of that year when my dad came home one night to despairingly report that the stores van had arrived from Crewe that afternoon with a consignment of desperately needed class '5' brake blocks amongst other items. When the fitters had unloaded the consignment they found the brake blocks to be unrecognisable - certainly not those that would fit a Stanier engine of any sort! The gaffer was called and when he saw the miscreant parts he realized with resigned despair that they were works leftovers from the long gone LNWR 'George V' class 4-4-0!

On occasions we would be visited at home by my father's predecessor, Ernest Crofts, by now an elderly gentleman who had been retired nearly 15 years. I overheard them chatting one afternoon in our front room lounge. My dad was regaling Ernest with the latest depressing goings on at 6B, when Ernest replied: 'Jack things are no worse now than when I was there, I used to cry with despair trying to keep the "Super Ds" running. There were always more jobs than there were engines available to handle them!' Well at least Ernest had escaped into a long and I believe happy retirement. Sometime during the last months of 1965 my father received notice that Mold Junction shed was to close in April the following year, this would leave him with just short of a year to serve before his retirement (he would be 65 on 7th March, 1967). Because of this he just resigned himself to the inevitable rundown that had started with the withdrawal notices served on any locomotive that was ready for a works overhaul. Such engines were deposited in sidings and their connecting rods were cut through to enable them to be towed to their execution at whatever scrap yard it had been agreed would purchase them.

The reader may recall that I had received two offers of an engineering apprenticeship, the first from Rolls Royce Aero Engines at Derby, the second from Hawker Siddeley Aviation near my home at Chester. Perhaps it was the 'old man upstairs' at work but in the event I chickened out of the Derby offer as it would have entailed living in digs on £4 5s. per week as against living at home on £3 6s. per week. It was fortunate for my mother that I took this decision. I have previously referred to something that I found troubling when out walking on Conway Mountain during the Christmas break in 1965 (see Chapter Nine), that uncharacteristically during that walk he seemed quiet and detached, also for some months he had been complaining of feeling a 'phantom' hair that played over one side of his face. Clearly there was nothing there yet the feeling kept recurring more and more frequently, he put it down to possible nerve damage resulting from his accident the previous year. One evening in January 1966 I arrived home from work to be greeted by my mother who upsettingly announced that my father had collapsed at work that day and had been admitted to hospital, where he had received an ECG amongst other tests. Apparently he had collapsed in his office and was discovered by driver Norman Barber* when he tried to enter his office and couldn't get the door open after knocking and getting no reply from within. He had fallen from his desk and was jammed behind the door, Norman immediately summoned help and I

---

* Norman was involved in the Baschurch accident (see Chapter Twelve).

J.E. Robinson (dad) was shed master at Mold Junction from May 1952 until closure in April 1966. He is seen here on a Sunday afternoon stroll on Saltney Cop in June 1965 in a typical pose with pipe in hand. Over the years his pipe and trilby hat became synonymous with his personality. A steam locomotive engineer to the bone his total dedication to the job was hardly matched by his rewards save for his personal satisfaction that a 6B engine was always a 'good 'un'. The fact that they went missing so often was testimony enough to this.　　　　　　　　　　　　　　　*Author*

believe he regained consciousness soon afterwards and an ambulance was called. He was released from hospital later that afternoon and when I arrived home at about 5.30 pm he was sitting up in bed reading the paper! 'What happened Dad?' I exclaimed, 'Don't really know', he replied, 'but I felt something in my face then that was it, must have blacked out!' My mum and I put it down to stress, possibly a nervous reaction following all the worry and aggravation of keeping things running these past months.

Sometime in the middle of that night I was awoken by my mum shaking me, 'Quick call Dr Fricker, I think your dad's having a fit!' When I entered their bedroom he was lying on the bed semi-conscious shaking violently with his face twitching in a most alarming way. The doctor duly arrived in his dressing gown and pyjamas; after preliminary pulse checks, etc., he administered an injection that had an immediate calming effect. He then questioned my mother about the events of the previous day and asked that I follow him back to his house where he had some tablets that should be taken orally every couple of hours. I grabbed some clothes and cycled up to his home a ¼ mile away; he told me that in the morning he would arrange a hospital admission for observation and that we should get him ready for picking up by ambulance. Well the next day dawned and by time I awoke my mother had him all ready for the ambulance which arrived after I had departed for work. That evening I visited him in Chester's City Hospital (now long gone) where he was sitting up in bed in reasonably good spirits. On questioning he just said that the same strange feeling had come back into his face followed by nothing, i.e. blacking out. To be honest he was more interested in how things were going with me as I was in my first year of year of apprenticeship in the company's training school, called the 'Tech School'.

Tests seemed to reveal very little about his ailment that was superficially at least responding to drugs, he was allowed home after a few days. My mother and I had decided that in the absence of anything more enlightening from the medical fraternity, nervous stress was the cause and we should keep his mind off anything to do with the shed or railways for the time being. I distinctly remember one Sunday afternoon when riding my bike past Saltney yard there was a line of engines all coupled up waiting to be towed to a scrapyard, probably Cashmores at Manchester, a couple of 'Halls', and a Stanier 2-8-0 plus a '38XX' 2-8-0. Normally on arrival home I would have reported such a sighting to my dad but believing that this might upset him or prompt a recurrence of those frightening convulsions, decided to keep my mouth shut. My mother even warned off visits from his work colleagues as she believed too that this would only serve to upset him.

January became February and by March he was making good progress and so accompanied me to the annual evening works' prize-giving ceremony. Here apprentices who had gained their qualifications in the previous summer's college exams would be presented with their degrees, diplomas or certificates from one of the company's 'big wigs', sometimes a retired Director or perhaps an existing executive from the Hatfield headquarters of Hawker Siddeley Aviation's De Havilland Division. My reason for attending was for the signing of indentures as for the intake of first year apprentices our six month probationary period was over and I had been granted an indenture for a five year engineering

Life as a shed master's son occasionally had its compensations, one in particular was the time which I was allowed to climb to the top of the coaling plant, accompanied by the running shift foreman, so that I could take this panoramic view of the shed and its yard in April 1966, unfortunately compromised by camera shake! 'Humpy' 0-6-0T No. 47598 is propelling a train of empty coal wagons across the scissors crossing. In the foregroundis the mechanised hoist of the ash plant, and to the left of the ash pit road are the narrow gauge skips stand in readiness for fires to be thrown out from the footplate. On the extreme right are two condemend '8F' class 2-8-0s, their connecting rods had been cut through and thrown into their empty tenders. This was the occasion of my dad's last visit to the shed.   *Author*

This picture of 'Black Five' class 4-6-0 No. 44990 of Mirfield shed was taken on the same day.
                              Author

apprenticeship that had to be signed by me and a parent or guardian. By the end of March my dad's health had improved considerably and despite the official closure notice that had decreed that on 18th April all activities at Mold Junction shed were to cease, he kept in touch with what was going on there by phone and by visits from his chief deputy the leading RSF Tom (Pensarn) Jones. The latter lived in nearby Saltney, but so called as he hailed originally from Pensarn to the immediate east of Llandudno Junction where he had attended Pensarn junior school with my mother many years earlier.

My father made his last visit to the shed on the Saturday morning of the last weekend of operation, I accompanied him and it was a bright and cold day. Unusually for me I took my camera and obtained several if somewhat poor quality shots, some of which are shown here. By that time there was very little activity save for the last remaining 'Humpy' No. 47598 that busied itself shunting coal and ash wagons twixt the shed and the East End yard opposite. A couple of class '5s' waiting on the end roads outside in the sunshine were the only engines remaining 'on shed', one of these, No. 44990, belonged to Mirfield shed in West Yorkshire. Over near the coaling plant on the wagon loop roads stood a couple of 6B's Stanier '8Fs', sadly condemned with their connecting rods cut through and thrown in their respective tenders; this rendered them useless for further work although fit for towing to the scrap yard. By lunchtime he had seen all that he wanted to see, we bade our farewells to the remaining staff shortly to be drafted to either Chester shed or perhaps Birkenhead and sadly we made our way home by bus. The following Monday morning the empty shed was filled with empty coal wagons and continued only as a signing-on point for the remainder of that year. The marshalling yards continued to operate with diesel shunters now being provided from Chester (ex-GWR) diesel depot. The firm impression that I got from all of the ex-6B men that I subsequently interviewed in the researching of this book 40 years later was that under Jack Robinson, Mold Junction was a 'happy shed' and the places that they were drafted to after closure did not even approach 6B for that level of contentedness, perceived or not! I don't think they were saying that just to please me as most left the railway shortly afterwards.

The Decline

My father's improvement in health was somewhat short-lived, within a few short weeks of his final visit to the shed his speech became slurred, mild at first but then it worsened and he found eating and holding a knife and fork more and more difficult. Soon he was unable to stand up unassisted and our GP ordered him back to hospital for further tests and observations. The whole process was taking an enormous toll on my mother who still believed that he was afflicted by some sort of nervous breakdown. For some unknown reason the medics did not come up with a plausible explanation and this was beginning to grate on me. After a move to what can best be described as a 'stroke re-hab unit' at the nearby Moston Hospital in May, from where he was allowed home at weekends, his condition seemed to stabilize somewhat.

A general view of Mold Junction shed in July 1996, compare this view with that on page 169 taken 32 years earlier.   *Author*

The remains of the ash pit emptying hoist at Mold Junction in 1996.   *Author*

Mold Junction shed offices in 1996 (under the Sandycroft road). The furthest arch still had what remains of the LNWR-style bay window frame common to all shed master's office windows. The middle arch was the stores and the nearest one, the enginemen's bothy.   *Author*

One piece of Mold Junction engine shed will continue to give service for generations to come. The 60 ft turntable has been expertly and beautifully restored to fully operational order and resited at Rowsley shed yard at Peak Rail's headquarters in Derbyshire.   *R. Carvell*

Early Days on the Festiniog Railway

At this time I was attending the Chester College of Further Education on day release and night school where I was studying for my ONC. Whilst there my interest in railways was brought to the attention of a certain engineering lecturer called Roy Goldstraw who was an active member of the Boston Lodge team of the Festiniog Railway (FR). Apparently Roy had a second home near Tan-y-Bwlch and periodically he would take working parties up to the works for weekends. I was invited one weekend in May 1966 and we were told to await picking up at the Northgate station in Chester. At that time the Chester Model Railway Club had its clubrooms on the station and Friday was the club night - so no problem there then! In due course Roy arrived in his green Ford 'Corsair' and picked up his three passengers, but not of course before some discourse with some of the club members on the latest developments on the layouts had been indulged in. What can only be described as a 'wild drive'of some 70 miles or so followed as Roy was no sluggard behind the wheel and by contemporary standards his 'V4' wasn't slow. The route via Bala and Trawsfynydd allowed our driver/host (during the last vestiges of daylight) to indulge in a running commentary on the route of the by then defunct Bala-Festiniog line, parts of which can still be seen today. His cottage was located in a miniscule hamlet called Rhyd up beyond TYB* and arrival was in darkness.

The following morning we cooked ourselves a good old English breakfast before setting out for the works replete with boots and overalls (no need for dayglo 'flak jackets' in those days). Our project was the roofing of the new style 'kit build' bogie coaches and my first duty was to accompany Roy across the Cob aboard the open Simplex petrol locomotive (later fitted with a cab roof and called *Mary Ann*). To say it was a touch breezy as we slogged across towing a bogie flat truck would not be an exaggeration! On arrival at Port† we ran onto the goods shed road, there to load up the roof materials for our weekend's work. (It's interesting to note that the goods shed later became the FR's museum and is now part of the main station facility.) We worked long and hard right through the day pausing only for cups of tea and coffee nailing up pre-cut plywood sheets over the roof trusses of a coach and then stretching over the weather-proof bitumen sheeting. There had not long before been some sort of open day event at the works and out in Glan-y-Mor yard stood one of the rusting and forlorn George England sister engines to *Prince*, *Palmerston* aptly adorned with a new wooden nameplate entitled 'Harold Wilson' - well if the cap fits! In those days the works was serenaded by an endless cacophony of Radio Caroline from an old radio set high in the rafters, coal was the indigenous fuel and the works boss was the ever present and laconic Paul Dukes, now sadly no longer with us. Oh yes, I almost forgot, the new station name board for Dduallt was prominently leaning against the wall at the entrance to the 'bothy' just to remind everybody what it was all about!

That first evening we packed in at about 5 pm and having 'washed up' repaired to a local hostelry at the village of Llanfrothen where a couple of pints went down without even touching the sides. Then it was back up the steep hill

---

* Tan-y-Bwlch or TYB as most society members found this abbreviation easier to pronounce!
† 'Port' was the Boston Lodge parlance for Portmadoc.

to Rhyd. Here the fourth member of our team who had joined us at lunchtime by train from Chester via the Blaenau Ffestiniog branch, an exemplary cook, prepared a massive bowl of spaghetti bolognese - most welcome! After that we all went by car down to TYB and then walked up the line to see the progress at Dduallt. What I saw on arrival there in the fading light well and truly mesmerized me! The true scale of the project to get the line back to Blaenau hit home, from that moment on I was infatuated with the Festiniog and several more working trips plus society membership followed and as they say 'the rest is history'!

On my return home that Sunday evening I greeted my dad who was enjoying one of his weekend visits home from hospital. My enthusiasm for what I had experienced that weekend was overflowing and together with some new promotional booklets that I had purchased at Portmadoc Harbour station I set about describing what I had seen and done. I made special reference to the civil engineering that was going on up at Dduallt in order to get the line up over the old tunnel and alongside the new pumped storage scheme lake. To my shock and utter disappointment he seemed totally disinterested; to think that only three years previously he and I had journeyed up to TYB from Portmadoc behind a 'Double Engine' and he was himself so enthusiastic about what he saw. This deflating experience only served to heighten my fear that there was something very seriously wrong with him and either the doctors were incompetent (as seemed unlikely) or weren't telling us something. A few more weekends passed then he became too ill to leave the hospital, I recall taking along my newly finished GEM model of a 'Prince' by now fully lined-out in LNWR livery and carrying the *Queen of the Belgians* nameplate and numbered 2396. This I have to say proudly livened him up somewhat and, although by now unable to talk, he gesticulated his friends to come and have a look at the model.

It was shortly afterwards that he descended into what can best be described as a half sleeping stupor. He spent his days slumped in a wheelchair and sometimes when awake cupped his forehead in his hand as if suffering a severe headache. His brother Arthur visited and immediately demanded that the registrar get him to a hospital that could correctly diagnose and treat his condition. The very next day he was ferried to Walton Hospital, Liverpool where various X-ray investigations were carried out. By the time we visited on the following Sunday courtesy of my mother's brother, Norman, he was in a permanent semi-comatose state. Here they informed us that the next day he would be transferred to Clatterbridge Hospital on the Wirral where he would subjected to a course of treatment but they wouldn't divulge what the cause was nor the treatment that would be meted out! In due course we arrived at the said establishment to find him lying in a ward bed with his head shaved and covered from his ears upwards in blue 'chalk' marks. Here two doctors, one I believe a consultant, took my mother and I into an ante-room and quietly explained that my father had a large inoperable vascular tumour stretching over the top of his brain. It was clear from their attitude that he was a 'goner' and the best they could do was to arrest its growth by 'deep x-ray' radiation treatment. I went crazy and demanded to know why it had taken them so long to determine what was wrong! As I recall they didn't give a clear answer which only served to inflame my feelings of the medical inadequacy; many years later one of my best friends (also a doctor) explained that any surgery at best would have rendered him a vegetable and at worst would have killed him. So there we had it; he endured a further week of x-ray treatment which in the event nearly killed him. We were called out one evening as the nurses didn't think he would make it through the night and thanks to a kind neighbour we got to the hospital (some 15 miles distant) in the early hours. He survived and was temporarily moved back to the City Hospital in Chester . Here over the final months of that miserably upsetting summer I, as a 17-year-old, was to witness my once intelligent and astringent father descend into an entirely vegetative state. Not an experience I would wish to visit on any youth of that age or older I can tell you.

His friend Max Dunn had relatives in Shavington near Crewe and he came to visit him and it has to be said was most upset by what he saw. It was late August and he offered to have me over for a short break 'to get away from it all'. The details of my break were described in Chapter Ten and throughout my time at Walberton discussion of my dad's condition was firmly off the agenda!

After about a month at the City Hospital he was moved to nearby Heath Lane Hospital in Broughton. This was effectively a geriatric hospital and to say that it upset my mum profoundly to see her husband of just 64 years of age lying in a ward amongst stroke-stricken men well into their 80s and older would be an understatement. Again he sort of stablized here and was visited by a number of his ex-Mold Junction shed staff along with his boss the DMPS Mr Walker Smith and his assistant Mr Thatcher. I found a library book on the 'North Western' and recall seeing his eyes sparkle for a few seconds when shown a picture of a 'Prince of Wales' class heading south from Rugby. That Christmas was probably the most miserable that I have ever spent either before or since. We had company at home from my grandmother and my aunt Sophie and her husband Victor Williams. But as they didn't possess a car we were dependent on neighbours to ferry us on Christmas Day to the hospital to see my father who by now, apart from odd 'waking' moments when he just stared with expressionless eyes not recognizing those around him, seemed to be in a permanent 'sleep'. My sister Ann was away in Canada with small children and so couldn't get home. One evening in late January my mother and I were summoned to his bedside by the duty staff nurse who believed that he wasn't going to make it through the night. I left later in the evening and my mother returned home in tears the following morning (25th January, 1967) to announce that he had passed away peacefully in the early hours with just a solitary tear rolling down his cheek to mark the end!

The Aftermath

The funeral was held at our local church, St Mark's in Saltney on the following Saturday morning and I think was attended by many of his shed staff as I recall the church being full. Afterwards the cortège with his close family travelled to Llangystenin near Llandudno Junction where he was interred in his father's grave. (Incorrectly, the gravestone gives his death as the 28th January.)

Looking back after all these years that last year of his life was such a trauma that I personally had become numbed by it all and the immediate effect of his death on my mother was, as one might expect, that of relief. She was desperately disappointed that having by then served the railway for 47 years he was denied his retirement. They had long planned their free time together do such things as taking rail trips into Europe, by then this facility had become allowable under the free pass scheme. However, the final 'kick in the teeth' came when she learned that, despite (in the late 1940s) backdating his payments into the staff superannuation scheme to ensure he had a full 20 years of contributions, unknown to her he had elected to maximize his pension by not allowing her a 50 per cent share in the event of his premature death (i.e. before 65 years). Like most people he believed that he would live well beyond the retiring age of 65. He died less than two months short of that date which meant my mother lost her railway pension rights and was just paid a gratuity which amounted to a lump sum of no more than what he had paid in contributions! This was a shock and bitter disappointment from which she never really recovered. For many years after, anything to do with the railway was sadly an anathema to her.

For my part it seemed that steam had also died with him: so much for his electrical engineer father's early admonishments of 'Why work with steam engines as they will soon be out of date and outmoded'! By August of the following year steam in the British Isles as a form of main line traction had passed into history and there passed a 20 year period when I lost most if not all of my interest in railways. Why with girlfriends and sports cars to maintain there was so much more to do after my student and apprenticeship days were over!

Memories of Saltney yard, the author's pencil sketch dates from 1964.

Acknowledgements

Norman Jones checks the proofs for the book *Holyhead's Royal Visit*.   *Author*

To my good friend the late Norman Jones FSCA of Warrington, who, because of his knowledge of my family history, inspired and encouraged the start of this work way back in 1995. The photograph (*above*) shows him checking proofs of our joint Foxline book about Queen Victoria's visit to Holyhead in 1900.

To fellow members of the LNWR Society for photographs from the J.M. Dunn Collection along with information, encouragement, and more, not forgetting Roger Carvell who sourced the photograph of the 'Venom' incident.

To my friend Greg Fox, who sadly passed away just prior to the publication of this book, for great encouragement and the three 'I's (information, inspiration and instruction).

To my pals from 6B including ex-fireman Cleve Jones, ex-drivers Bill Price and the late Emrys Williams and Idris Morris who supplied so much rich anecdotal information along with photographs, etc.

To my sister Ann Woodward who supplied information about my father's days at Llandudno Junction and her husband Ron who furnished information about his father, Herbert Woodward of Mouldsworth signal box. To Marya Lewis, daughter of my father's friend the late Joe Shervington, for detailed information and period photographs taken by her father.

To photographers Norman Kneale and Syd Wainwright who were able to supply so many valuable photographs portraying the local area during the period of my father's tenure at Mold Junction.

To my friends Norman Lee and David Goodwin of the Barrowmore Model Railway Club and its excellent Journal, whose continued encouragement and enthusiasm helped to see the project through to its conclusion.

Not forgetting Mike Bentley, John Dixon, Don Rowland and all those people too numerous to mention who sometimes (unwittingly) helped, if only in their positive reaction to what I was attempting to achieve with this work.

To my business partner and colleague Carolyn Carr who tirelessly assisted with office facilities whenever photocopying, proof reading etc., etc., was required.

Last but not least to my wife Gail who has put up with and supported me as well as supplying the 'midnight oil' to enable me to complete this work – eventually!